GREAT TASTES

INDIAN

First published in 2009 by Bay Books, an imprint of Murdoch Books Pty Limited
This edition published in 2010.

Murdoch Books Australia
Pier 8/9
23 Hickson Road
Millers Point NSW 2000
Phone: +61 (0) 2 8220 2000
Fax: +61 (0) 2 8220 2558
www.murdochbooks.com.au

Murdoch Books UK Limited
Erico House, 6th Floor
93–99 Upper Richmond Road
Putney, London SW15 2TG
Phone: +44 (0) 20 8785 5995
Fax: +44 (0) 20 8785 5985
www.murdochbooks.co.uk

Chief Executive: Juliet Rogers
Publishing Director: Kay Scarlett
Publisher: Lynn Lewis
Senior Designer: Heather Menzies
Designer: Wendy Inkster
Production: Kita George

ISBN: 9780681657755

PRINTED IN CHINA

IMPORTANT: Those who might be at risk from the effects of salmonella poisoning (the elderly, pregnant women, young children and those suffering from immune deficiency diseases) should consult their doctor with any concerns about eating raw eggs.

OVEN GUIDE: You may find cooking times vary depending on the oven you are using. For fan-forced ovens, as a general rule, set the oven temperature to 20°C (35°F) lower than indicated in the recipe.

GREAT TASTES

INDIAN

More than 120 easy recipes for every day

bay books

CONTENTS

SNACKS

SAMOSAS

MAKES 30

PASTRY
450 g (1 lb) maida or plain
   (all-purpose) flour
1 teaspoon salt
4 tablespoons oil or ghee

FILLING
400 g (14 oz) potatoes, cut into quarters
80 g (2 oz/½ cup) peas
1½ teaspoons cumin seeds
½ teaspoon coriander seeds
2 tablespoons oil
½ onion, finely chopped
¼ teaspoon ground turmeric
½ teaspoon garam masala
2 green chillies, chopped
3 cm (1¼ inch) piece of ginger, chopped
1½ tablespoons lemon juice
2 tablespoons chopped coriander
   (cilantro) leaves

oil, for deep-frying

1   To make the pastry, sift the maida and salt into a bowl, then rub in the oil or ghee until the mixture resembles breadcrumbs. Add 185 ml (6 fl oz/¾ cup) warm water to make a pliable dough. Turn out onto a floured surface and knead for 5 minutes, or until smooth. Cover and set aside for 15 minutes.

2   To make the filling, cook the potato in simmering water for 10 minutes, or until tender. Drain and cut into small cubes. Cook the peas in simmering water for 2 minutes. Drain and refresh in cold water.

3   Place a small frying pan over low heat, dry-roast the cumin seeds until aromatic, then remove. Dry-roast the coriander seeds. Grind ½ teaspoon of the cumin and all the coriander to a fine powder in a spice grinder or pestle and mortar.

4   Heat the oil in a heavy-based saucepan over low heat and fry the onion until light brown. Stir in all the cumin,

the coriander, turmeric and garam masala. Add the potato, chilli, ginger and stir for 1 minute. Mix in the lemon juice and coriander leaves and salt, to taste, then leave to cool.

5   On a floured surface, roll out a third of the pastry to a 28 cm (11 inch) circle, about 3 mm (⅛ inch) thick. Cut 10 circles with an 8 cm (3 inch) cutter and spoon ½ tablespoon of filling onto the centre of each. Moisten the edges with water, then fold over and seal with a fork into a semicircle. Repeat to use all the filling and pastry. Cover until ready to fry.

6   Fill a karhai or heavy-based saucepan one-third full with oil and heat to 180°C/350°F (a cube of bread will brown in 15 seconds). Fry a few samosas at a time until lightly browned. Turn them over and brown them on the other side. Drain on a wire rack for 5 minutes before draining on paper towels. Serve warm or cold. Seal them and use a fork to press the edges together firmly.

PORK TIKKA

SERVES 4

MARINADE

1 onion, roughly chopped

3 garlic cloves, roughly chopped

5 cm (2 inch) piece of ginger, roughly chopped

½ tablespoon ground cumin

1 teaspoon ground coriander

½ tablespoon garam masala

¼ teaspoon chilli powder

½ pinch ground black pepper

250 ml (9 fl oz/1 cup) thick plain yoghurt

SAUCE

1 large red onion, roughly chopped

1 garlic clove, roughly chopped

2.5 cm (1 inch) piece of ginger, roughly chopped

1 green chilli, roughly chopped

25 g (1 oz/¾ cup) coriander (cilantro) leaves

500 g (1 lb 2 oz) pork tenderloin, centre cut, cut into 2.5 cm (1 inch) cubes

125 ml (4 fl oz/½ cup) oil

1 tablespoon garam masala

1 **To prepare the marinade,** finely chop the onion, garlic and ginger in a food processor or, if you don't have a processor, with a knife. Add the spices and yoghurt to the paste and mix through.

2 **Put the pork in a bowl,** add the marinade and mix well. Cover and marinate in the fridge for 2 hours or overnight.

3 **To make the sauce,** finely chop the onion, garlic, ginger, chilli and coriander in a food processor or, if you don't have a processor, with a knife.

4 **Heat the oil** in a heavy-based frying pan, large enough to fit the meat in a single layer, until sizzling but not smoking. Add the sauce and stir over medium heat for 2 minutes, or until softened but not brown. Increase the heat to high and add the pork with the marinade. Stir constantly for 5 minutes, then reduce the heat to medium and let the meat and its juices bubble away for 15–20 minutes, or until the liquid has completely evaporated. The meat and the dryish sauce will be a rich dark brown.

5 **Season with salt,** to taste, and sprinkle with the garam masala. Cook for another 2 minutes to allow the added seasoning to be absorbed.

TANDOORI PANEER

SERVES 4

300 g (11 oz) paneer

2 green capsicums (peppers)

1 onion

2 firm tomatoes

310 ml (10¾ fl oz/1¼ cups) thick plain yoghurt

1 teaspoon ground turmeric

2 cm (¾ inch) piece of ginger, grated

4 garlic cloves, crushed

1½ tablespoons lemon juice

2 tablespoons chopped mint leaves

1 tablespoon chopped coriander (cilantro) leaves

2 tablespoons oil

1 Cut the paneer into pieces measuring about 2 x 1.5 cm (¾ x ⅝ inch). Cut the capsicums into squares, the onion into chunks and the tomatoes into cubes. Mix the yoghurt, turmeric, ginger, garlic and lemon juice, together with a little salt, in a large bowl. Stir in the herbs. Add the paneer and vegetables, cover and refrigerate for 3 hours.

2 Preheat the grill (broiler) to its highest setting. Using 8 skewers, thread onto each 5 pieces of paneer and some capsicum, onion and tomato. Brush with the oil, season with salt and grill (broil) on all sides for 3–4 minutes, or until the paneer and vegetables are cooked and slightly charred around the edges. Serve with roti and a salad such as laccha.

NIMKI

MAKES 60

50 g (1¾ oz/2 cups) maida or plain (all-purpose) flour

1 teaspoon salt

1 teaspoon kalonji (nigella seeds)

1 tablespoon ghee

oil, for deep-frying

1 Sift the maida and salt into a bowl and add the kalonji. Rub in the ghee until the mixture resembles breadcrumbs. Add about 125 ml (4 fl oz/½ cup) water, a little at a time, to make a pliable dough. Turn the dough out onto a floured surface and knead for 5 minutes, or until smooth, then cover and rest it for 10 minutes. Don't refrigerate the dough or the ghee will harden.

2 Divide the dough into two portions and roll out each portion until about 3 mm (⅛ inch) thick. Cut into 1 cm (½ inch) wide strips, then into diamonds 3 cm (1¼ inches) long, by making diagonal cuts along the strips. Prick the diamonds with a fork.

3 Fill a karhai or heavy-based saucepan one-third full with oil and heat to about 170°C/325°F (a cube of bread will brown in 20 seconds).

4 Fry the nimki in batches until light golden and crisp. Drain on paper towels. Serve with mint and coriander chutney.

CHUCUMBER

SERVES 4

1 red onion, finely chopped

2 small cucumbers, about 200 g (7 oz), finely chopped

100 g (3½ oz) ripe tomatoes, finely chopped

3 tablespoons finely chopped coriander (cilantro)

1 red chilli, finely chopped

1 green chilli, finely chopped

1½ tablespoons lemon juice

1 teaspoon oil

125 g (4½ oz/¾ cup) unroasted peanuts, roughly chopped

1 teaspoon salt

½ teaspoon ground black pepper

1½ teaspoons chaat masala

1 **Stir together** in a bowl the onion, cucumber, tomato, coriander, chillies and lemon juice.

2 **Heat the oil in a heavy-based frying pan** over high heat, add the peanuts and salt and fry for 1 minute. Sprinkle with the pepper and chaat masala and stir. Fry for 2 minutes. Remove from the heat and add to the onion mixture.

3 **Season with more salt,** to taste, just before serving. The seasoning is added at the end to prevent the ingredients releasing too much juice before serving.

4 **Serve in small bowls.** Chucumber can be eaten with a spoon or scooped up in pieces of roti or poppadoms.

SPICY WHITEBAIT

SERVES 4

300 g (10½ oz) whitebait

½ teaspoon chilli powder

¼ teaspoon cayenne pepper

½ teaspoon ground turmeric

oil, for deep-frying

1 Rinse the whitebait and dry them thoroughly on paper towels. Mix the chilli powder, cayenne pepper and turmeric together and toss the whitebait in the seasoning until well coated.

2 Fill a karhai or heavy-based saucepan one-third full with oil and heat to 190°C/375°F (a cube of bread will brown in 10 seconds). Fry the fish in batches until crisp, drain on paper towels and sprinkle with salt. Serve hot and crisp.

GOLDEN EGG CURRY

SERVES 4

8 eggs

oil, for deep-frying

2 ripe tomatoes

25 g (1 oz) ghee

1 onion, finely chopped

1 garlic clove, finely chopped

420 ml (14½ fl oz/1⅔ cups) coconut milk

1 teaspoon ground turmeric

½ teaspoon cayenne pepper

6 curry leaves

1 **Put the eggs in a saucepan** of water and bring to the boil. Boil for about 6 minutes, until medium-hard, then cool quickly in a bowl of cold water. Shell them. You can now deep-fry the eggs if you wish. Fill a karhai or heavy-based saucepan one-third full with oil and heat to about 170°C/325°F (a cube of bread will brown in 20 seconds). Fry the eggs in batches until golden and crisp. Drain on paper towels. Cut each egg in half if you prefer.

2 **Score a cross in the top of each tomato.** Plunge into boiling water for 20 seconds, then drain and peel away from the cross. Roughly chop the tomatoes, discarding the cores and seeds.

3 **Melt the ghee** in a karhai or heavy-based frying pan over low heat, add the onion and garlic and cook until soft and golden. Add the tomato and cook until soft. Gradually stir in the coconut milk, then the turmeric, cayenne and season with salt. Bring to the boil and simmer for 2–3 minutes, until the sauce thickens slightly. Add the eggs and heat gently for 2–3 minutes. Garnish with curry leaves.

PARSI SCRAMBLED EGGS

SERVES 4

2 tablespoons oil or ghee

1 red onion, finely chopped

1 garlic clove, finely chopped

2 cm (¾ inch) piece of ginger, grated

1 teaspoon garam masala

pinch of chilli powder

4 strands saffron soaked in
   2 tablespoons hot milk

6 eggs

2 green chillies, finely chopped

4 slices of toast

chopped coriander (cilantro) leaves

1 **Heat the oil** or ghee in a heavy-based saucepan over low heat, add the onion and garlic and fry for 4–5 minutes, until soft. Add the ginger and stir for 2 minutes, or until soft. Add the garam masala, chilli powder and saffron and cook for 1 minute. Season with salt.

2 **Whisk the eggs** and add them to the saucepan. Cook over low heat, scraping the egg from the side of the pan into the centre until the mixture is soft and creamy. Remove from the heat because the eggs will continue cooking. Sprinkle the chopped chilli over the egg, then fold in. Pile onto hot toast, sprinkle with chopped coriander and serve.

BHEL PURI

SERVES 6

MINT CHUTNEY

50 g (1¾ oz) coriander leaves

50 g (1¾ oz) mint leaves

6 garlic cloves, chopped

3 red chillies, chopped

½ red onion, chopped

3 tablespoons lemon juice

TAMARIND CHUTNEY

60 g (2¼ oz) fennel seeds

440 ml (15¼ fl oz/1¾ cups) tamarind purée

100 g (3½ oz) ginger, sliced

300 g (10½ oz/1²/₃ cups) soft brown sugar

1 teaspoon chilli powder

1 tablespoon ground cumin

1 tablespoon chaat masala

1 teaspoon black salt

3 potatoes

1 tomato

120 g (4¼ oz) puffed rice

60 g (2¼ oz) sev (besan flour) noodles

1 green unripe mango, sliced into thin slivers

1 onion, finely chopped

4 tablespoons finely chopped coriander (cilantro) or mint leaves

1 teaspoon chaat masala

12 crushed puri crisps

1 **To make the mint chutney,** blend the ingredients together in a food processor or pestle and mortar. Transfer to a saucepan and bring to the boil. Remove from the heat, leave to cool, then season with salt.

2 **To make the tamarind chutney,** place a small frying pan over low heat and dry-roast the fennel until aromatic. Mix together the tamarind, ginger, sugar and 250 ml (1 cup) water in a saucepan. Cook over low heat until the tamarind blends into the mixture and the sugar completely dissolves.

3 **Strain out the ginger** and cook the remaining mixture to a thick pulp. Add the fennel seeds, chilli powder, cumin, chaat masala and black salt. Season with salt and reduce, stirring occasionally, over medium heat until thickened to a dropping consistency (it will fall in sheets off the spoon). Leave to cool.

4 **To make** the bhel puri, cook the potatoes in boiling water for 10 minutes or until tender, then cut into small cubes. Score a cross in the top of the tomato. Plunge into boiling water for 20 seconds, then drain and peel. Roughly chop the tomato, discarding the core and seeds and reserving any juices.

5 **Put the puffed rice,** noodles, mango, onion, chopped coriander, chaat masala and puri crisps in a large bowl and toss them together. When well mixed, stir in a little of each chutney. Vary the chutney amounts depending on the flavour you want to achieve. The tamarind chutney has a tart flavour and the mint chutney is hot. Serve in small bowls and garnish with coriander leaves.

Note: Leftover mint chutney can be eaten with samosas or pakoras but cannot be stored. Store unused tamarind chutney in a jar in the fridge. It will keep for several weeks.

LAMB KOFTA

SERVES 6

1 small onion, roughly chopped

5 cm (2 inch) piece of ginger, roughly chopped

2 garlic cloves, roughly chopped

2 green chillies, seeded and roughly chopped

15 g (½ oz) coriander (cilantro) leaves

2 tablespoons thick plain yoghurt

500 g (1 lb 2 oz) minced (ground) lamb

2½ teaspoons ground cumin

1½ teaspoons ground coriander

2 teaspoons garam masala

¼ teaspoon chilli powder

2½ teaspoons salt

½ teaspoon ground black pepper

3–4 tablespoons oil

1   Blend the onion, ginger, garlic, chopped chilli and the coriander leaves together in a food processor until they form a paste. If you don't have a food processor, use a pestle and mortar, or finely chop everything together with a knife. Add the yoghurt to the paste and mix well.

2   Put the lamb mince in a bowl, add the paste and mix by hand, kneading the ingredients into the meat until thoroughly combined. Add all the spices, and the salt and pepper, and mix again to distribute evenly. Cover and refrigerate for 1–2 hours to allow the flavours to develop and also to make the mixture firmer and therefore easier to handle.

3   Wet your hands and roll small handfuls (about a heaped tablespoon) of the mince mixture into small balls (wetting your hands prevents the mixture sticking to your hands). You should have about 30–40 meatballs.

4   Heat 1 tablespoon of the oil in a large, heavy-based frying pan. When hot but not smoking,

5   Add 10 meatballs in a single layer. Brown on all sides by gently shaking the pan for 2–3 minutes. Don't be tempted to turn them over with a spoon or they may break up. Test a kofta by breaking it open. If it is cooked through, there should be no pink meat inside. If the meat is still pink, cook for another minute or two. Remove and drain on paper towels. Repeat with the remaining meatballs. Serve with cocktail sticks for picking them up. Mint and coriander chutney is the perfect accompaniment but other chutneys are also suitable.

ALOO KI TIKKI

MAKES 24

500 g (1 lb 2 oz) potatoes, cut into pieces

150 g (5½ oz/1 cup) fresh or frozen peas

4 tablespoons oil

2 green chillies, finely chopped

½ red onion, finely chopped

2 cm (¾ inch) piece of ginger, grated

1 teaspoon ground turmeric

1 teaspoon ground cumin

1 teaspoon ground coriander

½ teaspoon garam masala

2 tablespoons besan (chickpea flour)

1 tablespoon lemon juice

1 Cook the potatoes in boiling water for 15 minutes, or until tender enough to mash. Drain well until they are dry but still hot. Cook the peas in boiling water for 4 minutes, or until tender, then drain.

2 Mash the potato in a large bowl and add the peas. Put 1 tablespoon of the oil in a small saucepan and fry the chilli, onion, ginger and spices for 1 minute, or until aromatic. Add them to the potato with the besan flour and mix. Mix in the lemon juice and some salt. Divide the potato into portions the size of golf balls and shape into patties.

3 Heat the remaining oil in a heavy-based frying pan (non-stick if you have one) and add the potato patties in batches. Fry them on each side until crisp and golden brown. Serve hot or cold in small dishes.

ALOO CHAAT

SERVES 4

1 kg (2 lb 4 oz) small salad potatoes, unpeeled

80 ml (2½ oz/⅓ cup) tamarind purée

4 green chillies, seeded and finely chopped

4 tablespoons chopped coriander (cilantro) leaves

2 teaspoons chaat masala

1 **Boil the potatoes** in their skins for 15 minutes, or until just tender. Peel the potatoes and slice them into small rounds. Put them in a serving bowl.

2 **Mix the tamarind purée** with 2 tablespoons water. Mix all the other ingredients with the tamarind, then season with salt.

3 **Gently toss the potato rounds** with the tamarind mixture and serve as a snack or as a refreshing salad on a very hot day.

KACHORIS

MAKES 20

FILLING
100 g (3½ oz) urad dal

1½ tablespoons oil

1 teaspoon cumin seeds

¼ teaspoon ground turmeric

¼ teaspoon asafoetida

3 green chillies, finely chopped (optional)

2 cm (¾ inch) piece of ginger, grated

DOUGH
200 g (7 oz) atta (chapati flour), or 100 g (3½ oz) wholemeal flour, mixed with 100 g (3½ oz) maida or plain (all-purpose) flour

1 teaspoon kalonji (nigella seeds)

2 teaspoons oil or ghee

oil, for deep-frying

1   **To make the filling,** soak the dal in 500 ml (17 fl oz/2 cups) cold water for 2 hours. Drain and chop in a food processor for a few seconds to form a coarse paste. If you don't have a food processor, grind the dal in a pestle and mortar. Heat the oil over medium heat in a saucepan, add the cumin seeds, then cover and allow the seeds to pop. Add the turmeric, asafoetida, chilli and ginger and stir until well mixed. Add the dal paste and 125 ml (4 fl oz/½ cup) water and cook over low heat, stirring constantly until the liquid has evaporated. Add salt, to taste. Spread on a plate and leave until cold.

2   **To make the dough,** sift the atta and a little salt into a bowl and add the kalonji. Rub in the oil or ghee until the mixture resembles breadcrumbs. Add 125–170 ml (½–²/₃ cup) warm water, a little at a time, to make a pliable dough. Turn out onto a floured surface and knead for 5 minutes, or until the dough is smooth. Cover and set aside for 15 minutes.

3   **Divide the dough** into 20 balls. Roll one out on a floured surface to resemble a thin pancake 8–10 cm (3–4 inches) in diameter. Place 1 heaped teaspoon of the dal mixture in the centre, then fold over the dough to form into a semicircle. Pinch the edges together to seal securely. Gently roll out on a floured surface, taking care that the filling doesn't ooze out. Try to retain the semicircular shape. Repeat to use all the dough and filling.

4   **Fill a karhai** or heavy-based saucepan one-third full with oil and heat to 180°C/350°F (a cube of bread will brown in 15 seconds). Lower a kachori into the hot oil and, when it rises to the surface, gently push it down using the back of a spoon, to keep it submerged until it puffs up. Turn it over and cook until the other side is lightly browned. Drain on a wire rack.

PRAWN PAKORAS

MAKES 30

600 g (1 lb 5 oz) prawns (shrimp)

50 g (1¾ oz/½ cup) besan (chickpea flour)

1 large red onion, finely chopped

1 teaspoon dried pomegranate seeds

4 green chillies, seeded and finely chopped

2 tablespoons finely chopped coriander (cilantro) leaves

pinch of bicarbonate of soda (baking soda)

ghee or oil, for deep-frying

1 **Peel and devein the prawns,** then cut into small pieces. Put the besan flour in a bowl and add 2 tablespoons of water, or enough to make a thick batter, mixing with a fork to beat out any lumps. Add the remaining ingredients, except the oil, to the batter, season with salt and mix well.

2 **Fill a karhai or heavy-based saucepan** one-third full with ghee or oil and heat to 180°C/350°F (a cube of bread will brown in 15 seconds). Drop 1 heaped teaspoon of batter at a time into the ghee or oil and deep-fry in lots of six or eight pakoras until they are brown all over. Remove and drain on paper towels. Serve hot.

GOLL BHAJI

MAKES 20

90 g (3¼ oz/½ cup) rice flour

50 g (1¾ oz/⅓ cup) cashew nuts

75 g (2½ oz/⅔ cup) besan (chickpea flour)

pinch of bicarbonate of soda (baking soda)

10 curry leaves, chopped

4 green chillies, seeded and finely chopped

2 cm (¾ inch) piece of ginger, finely chopped

1 red onion, finely chopped

1 tablespoon ghee

oil, for deep-frying

1   Place a small frying pan over low heat and dry-roast the rice flour until it turns light brown. Dry-roast the cashew nuts in the same pan until they brown, then finely chop them. Mix the rice flour with the besan flour, then add the bicarbonate of soda and a pinch of salt. Add the cashew nuts, curry leaves, green chilli, ginger, onion and ghee. Mix together well, adding a few drops of water, if necessary, to make a stiff dough. Form into 20 small balls.

2   Fill a karhai or heavy-based saucepan one-third full with ghee or oil and heat to 180°C/350°F (a cube of bread will brown in 15 seconds). Fry five or six balls at a time until golden brown, then drain each batch on paper towels.

KASHMIRI LAMB CUTLETS

SERVES 6

1 kg (2 lb 4 oz) lamb cutlets
¾ teaspoon cumin seeds
1 teaspoon coriander seeds
¾ teaspoon black peppercorns
500 ml (17 fl oz/2 cups) milk
2 cinnamon sticks
10 cardamom seeds
10 cloves
2 cm (¾ inch) piece of ginger, grated
2 onions, finely chopped
75 g (2½ oz/⅔ cup) besan (chickpea flour)
2 teaspoons chilli powder
125 ml (4 fl oz/½ cup) thick plain yoghurt
oil, for deep-frying
lime quarters, to serve

1 Trim the lamb of any fat and scrape the bone ends clean. Place a small frying pan over low heat and dry-roast the cumin seeds until aromatic. Remove them and dry-roast the coriander seeds. Crush the coriander and cumin seeds with the peppercorns in a spice grinder or pestle and mortar. Transfer to a large, heavy-based saucepan and add the milk, cinnamon, cardamom, cloves, ginger and onion. Bring to the boil over medium heat, then add the chops to the pan and return to the boil. Reduce the heat and simmer for 30 minutes, or until the meat is tender and very little liquid remains. Remove the cutlets and drain them.

2 Whisk the besan flour and chilli powder into the yoghurt with 60 ml (2 fl oz/¼ cup) water, to make a batter.

3 Fill a karhai or heavy-based saucepan one-third full of oil and heat to 180°C/350°F (a cube of bread will brown in 15 seconds). Dip the cutlets in the batter, shake off any excess, then fry them in batches in the hot oil until they are crisp. Drain on paper towels and keep them warm. Serve sprinkled with a little lime juice and salt, to taste.

CHILLI LAMB CUTLETS

MAKES 8

8 lamb cutlets

¼ teaspoon chilli powder

½ teaspoon ground turmeric

1 teaspoon garam masala

2 cm (¾ inch) piece of ginger, grated

1 garlic clove, crushed

1 tablespoon thick plain yoghurt

3 tablespoons lemon juice

1　**Trim the lamb** of any fat and scrape the bone ends clean. Mix together the remaining ingredients to form a paste, adding a little of the lemon juice if necessary. Rub the paste over the chops, then cover and refrigerate for 2 hours or overnight.

2　**Preheat the grill** (broiler) to its highest setting. Sprinkle the chops with salt on both sides and grill (broil) them on each side for 2–3 minutes, or until they are browned and sizzling. Squeeze the remaining lemon juice over them before serving.

VEGETABLE BHAJI

MAKES 20

100 g (3½ oz) carrots

100 g (3½ oz) snowpeas (mangetout)

50 g (1¾ oz) thin eggplants (aubergines)

220 g (7¾ oz/2¼ cups) besan (chickpea flour)

1 teaspoon chilli powder

1 teaspoon ground turmeric

¼ teaspoon asafoetida

6 curry leaves

oil, for deep-frying

1 Cut the vegetables into thin sticks. Mix together the besan flour, chilli powder, turmeric, asafoetida and a pinch of salt. Add enough water to make a thick batter that will hold the vegetables together. Mix the vegetables and curry leaves into the batter.

2 Fill a karhai or heavy-based saucepan one-third full with oil and heat to 180°C/350°F (a cube of bread will brown in 15 seconds). Lift clumps of vegetables out of the batter and lower carefully into the oil. Fry until golden all over and cooked through, then drain on paper towels. Sprinkle with salt and serve hot with chutney or raita.

MASALA VADA

MAKES 18

100 g (3½ oz) urad dal

120 g (4 oz) chana dal

2 green chillies, seeded and
 finely chopped

8 curry leaves, roughly chopped

½ teaspoon fennel seeds, crushed

1 red onion, finely chopped

½ teaspoon garam masala

3 tablespoons grated coconut

3 cm (1¼ inch) piece of ginger, grated

4 tablespoons chopped coriander
 (cilantro) leaves

3 tablespoons rice flour or urad dal flour

pinch of baking powder (optional)

oil, for deep-frying

1   Soak the dal in cold water for 4 hours, then drain. Reserve 2 tablespoons of the soaked dal and coarsely grind the remainder in a food processor or pestle and mortar. Add the reserved dal to the ground dal for texture. Add the chillies, curry leaves, fennel, onion, garam masala, coconut, ginger and coriander leaves. Mix well and season with salt. Add the flour and baking powder, if using (it gives a crisper texture), then mix until the texture is soft but the dough can be shaped (you may need to add a little water). Divide the mixture into 18 portions and form each into a ball. Slightly flatten each ball to form a patty.

2   Fill a karhai or heavy-based saucepan one-third full with oil and heat to 180°C/350°F (a cube of bread will brown in 15 seconds). Fry the patties in the hot oil, in batches of four or five, until golden brown and crisp. Drain well on paper towels and serve hot with a chutney.

SINGHARAS

MAKES 24

PASTRY

250 g (9 oz/2 cups) maida or plain (all-purpose) flour

2 tablespoons ghee

MEAT FILLING

4 ripe tomatoes

2 tablespoons ghee or oil

2 cinnamon sticks

6 cloves

1 cardamom pod

3 green chillies, chopped

1 large onion, finely chopped

3–4 curry leaves

4 garlic cloves, crushed

1 teaspoon ground turmeric

5 cm (2 inch) piece of ginger, grated

500 g (1 lb 2 oz) minced (ground) lamb

150 g (5½ oz/1 cup) peas

1 teaspoon garam masala

oil, for deep-frying

1   To make the pastry, sift the maida and a pinch of salt into a bowl. Rub in the ghee until the mixture resembles breadcrumbs. Add 125 ml (4 fl oz/½ cup) warm water, a little at a time, to make a pliable dough. Turn onto a floured surface and knead for 5 minutes on a floured surface, or until the dough is smooth. Cover and set aside for 30 minutes.

2   To make the meat filling, score a cross in the top of each tomato. Plunge into boiling water for 20 seconds, drain and peel away from the cross, then roughly chop, discarding the cores and seeds and reserving any juices. Heat the ghee or oil in a karhai or large saucepan over low heat and fry the cinnamon, cloves, cardamom and chilli. Add the onion, curry leaves, garlic, turmeric and ginger and fry for 5 minutes, or until the onion is brown. Add the lamb, fry until brown, then add the tomato and cover with a tight lid. Cook gently, stirring occasionally until the lamb is tender. Add the peas, cover and cook for 5 minutes. If there is any liquid left, turn up the heat and let it evaporate. Remove the whole spices. Season with salt, to taste, and sprinkle with garam masala.

3   Divide the dough into 12 portions, roll out each to a 12 cm (5 inch) circle, then cut each circle in half. Take one piece and form a hollow cone by folding the dough in half and sealing the two edges of the cut side together. It is easiest to wet one edge and make a small overlap. Fill three-quarters full with filling. Don't overfill. Seal the top edges, then pinch to give a fluted finish. Repeat with the remaining dough and filling.

4   Fill a karhai or heavy-based saucepan one-third full with oil and heat to 180°C/350°F (a cube of bread will brown in 15 seconds). Deep-fry the singharas in batches until well browned. Drain on a wire rack and keep warm.

BANANA CHIPS

SERVES 8

10 small green bananas
oil, for deep-frying
1 tablespoon salt
ground turmeric (optional)

1 Before you start, oil your hands or put on disposable gloves as a thick, sticky sap will be given off by the unripe bananas. Using a knife or mandolin, cut the bananas into 5 mm (¼ inch) thick slices, oiling the blade if it gets sticky.

2 Fill a karhai or heavy-based saucepan one-third full with oil and heat to 180°C/350°F (a cube of bread will brown in 15 seconds). Put the sliced bananas directly into the hot oil in batches and stir while the chips cook. After 1 or 2 minutes, put in a teaspoon of salt (the oil will not splutter). You will need to do this for the first batch, then for every second batch.

3 Remove the banana chips when golden brown, drain on paper towels and toss them in some ground turmeric.

4 Store the banana chips in an airtight container when they are completely cold. If the chips are not cooled completely, they will go soggy. The chips will keep for 2 weeks but may need refreshing after 10 days. Do this by heating them in a hot oven, or under a grill (broiler), until they are crisp.

RASAM

SERVES 4

3 tablespoons tamarind purée

1½ tablespoons coriander seeds

2 tablespoons cumin seeds

1 tablespoon black peppercorns

1 tablespoon oil

5 garlic cloves, skins on, roughly pounded

1 red onion, thinly sliced

2–3 dried chillies, torn into pieces

2 stalks curry leaves

200 g (7 oz) skinless, boneless chicken thighs, cut into small pieces

1 **Mix the tamarind purée** with 750 ml (26 fl oz/3 cups) water. Place a small frying pan over low heat and dry-roast the coriander seeds until aromatic. Remove, then dry-roast the cumin seeds, followed by the black peppercorns. Grind them together using a spice grinder or a pestle and mortar.

2 **Heat the oil in a large,** heavy-based saucepan over low heat, add the garlic and onion and fry until golden. Add the chilli and the curry leaves and fry for 2 minutes, or until they are aromatic. Add the tamarind water, the ground spices and season with salt. Bring to the boil, reduce the heat and simmer for 10 minutes.

3 **Add the chicken to the saucepan** with 250 ml (9 fl oz/ 1 cup) water and simmer for 20 minutes, gradually adding another 250 ml (9 fl oz/1 cup) water as the soup reduces. Remove any garlic skin which has floated to the top. Season with salt, to taste. Serve with rice.

TAMATAR SHORBA

SERVES 4

2 tablespoons oil

1 onion, finely chopped

3 Indian bay leaves (cassia leaves)

5 cm (2 inch) cinnamon stick

12 peppercorns

2 teaspoons ground cumin

2 teaspoons garam masala

800 g (1 lb 12 oz) tinned chopped tomatoes

1 teaspoon sugar

250 ml (9 fl oz/1 cup) chicken stock

coriander (cilantro) leaves

1 Heat the oil over low heat in a heavy-based saucepan and fry the onion, bay leaves, cinnamon and peppercorns until the onion is soft. Add the cumin, garam masala and the tomato, mashing the tomatoes with a fork to break them up. Add the sugar and stock and slowly bring to the boil. Simmer over low heat for 30 minutes.

2 Strain the soup by pushing it through a sieve, using the back of a metal spoon to push against the solids and extract as much of the liquid as possible. Discard what's left in the sieve. Reheat, then season with salt, to taste, and garnish with the coriander leaves before serving.

SAMBHAR

225 g (8 oz/¾ cup) toor dal (yellow lentils)

2 tablespoons coriander seeds

10 black peppercorns

½ teaspoon fenugreek seeds

2 tablespoons grated coconut

1 tablespoon roasted chana dal

6 dried chillies

2 drumsticks, cut into 5 cm (2 inch) pieces

2 carrots, cubed

1 onion, roughly chopped

125 g (4½ oz) eggplants (aubergines), cubed

50 g (1¾ oz) small okra, topped and tailed

1 tablespoon tamarind purée

2 tablespoons oil

1 teaspoon black mustard seeds

10 curry leaves

½ teaspoon ground turmeric

½ teaspoon asafoetida

1 Soak the dal in 500 ml (17 fl oz/2 cups) water for 2 hours. Drain the dal and put them in a saucepan with 1 litre (35 fl oz/ 4 cups) of water. Bring to the boil, then skim off any scum from the surface. Cover and simmer for 2 hours, or until the dal is cooked and tender.

2 Place a small frying pan over low heat and dry-roast the coriander, peppercorns, fenugreek, coconut, chana dal and chillies, stirring constantly until the coconut is golden brown. Grind the roasted mixture to a fine powder using a pestle and mortar or a spice grinder.

3 Bring 750 ml (26 fl oz/3 cups) water to the boil in a saucepan. Add the pieces of drumstick and the cubed carrot and bring back to the boil. Simmer for 10 minutes, then add the onion, eggplant and okra and more water if necessary. Simmer until the vegetables are almost cooked.

4 Put the boiled dal and their liquid, the ground spices, the vegetables (with any vegetable water) and tamarind in a large saucepan and bring slowly to the boil. Reduce the heat and simmer for 30 minutes. Season with salt, to taste.

5 Heat the oil in a small saucepan over medium heat, add the mustard seeds, cover and shake the pan until they start to pop. Add the curry leaves, turmeric, asafoetida and a little salt. Pour onto the simmering dal and stir until well mixed.

SEAFOOD

PATRA NI MACCHI

SERVES 4

4 x 500 g (1 lb 2 oz) pomfret, sole or
   leatherjacket fillets, skinned

young banana leaves

1 teaspoon ground cumin

½ teaspoon sugar

150 g (5½ oz) grated coconut

4 green chillies, seeded and chopped

4 tablespoons chopped coriander
   (cilantro) leaves

a few mint leaves

6 garlic cloves, chopped

1 green unripe mango, diced

3 tablespoons oil or ghee

3 tablespoons lime or lemon juice

mint leaves, to garnish

whole green chillies, to serve

1 **Wash the fish fillets,** pat dry and cut into 8 cm (3 inch) pieces. Cut the banana leaves into as many 23 cm (9 inch) squares as there are pieces of fish (you should have about six to eight). Soften the banana leaves by dipping them into a pan of very hot water. Wipe the pieces dry as they become pliant. If you can't get banana leaves, use foil.

2 **Grind the cumin,** sugar, coconut, chilli, coriander, mint, garlic and green mango to a paste in a food processor, blender or pestle and mortar. Heat 1 tablespoon of the oil or ghee in a frying pan and cook the paste over low heat until aromatic. Season with salt.

3 **Place the banana leaf squares** on a work surface. Apply the paste liberally to both sides of each piece of fish. Sprinkle some lime or lemon juice on the fish. Place a piece of fish on each banana leaf and wrap up like a parcel, tying them firmly with kitchen string.

4 **Using a large,** heavy-based frying pan which has a lid, heat the remaining oil or ghee and shallow-fry the fish parcels together on one side. After about 5 minutes, turn the parcels over and fry for another 5 minutes. The leaves will darken and shrink. Cover the pan and cook the fish for a few more minutes.

5 **Open out each fish parcel** on its plate. Garnish with mint leaves and green chilli 'flowers' (do this by making slits down into the chilli from the top towards the stem so you form strips which fan out).

BOMBAY-STYLE FISH

SERVES 4

2 garlic cloves, crushed

3 small green chillies, seeded and finely chopped

½ teaspoon ground turmeric

½ teaspoon ground cloves

½ teaspoon ground cinnamon

½ teaspoon ground cayenne pepper

1 tablespoon tamarind purée

170 ml (5½ fl oz/⅔ cup) oil

800 g (1 lb 12 oz) pomfret, sole or leatherjacket fillets, skinned

310 ml (10¾ fl oz/1¼ cups) coconut cream

2 tablespoons chopped coriander (cilantro) leaves

1 **Mix together the garlic,** chilli, spices, tamarind and 125 ml (4 fl oz/½ cup) of the oil. Place the fish fillets in a shallow dish and spoon the marinade over them. Turn the fish over, cover and refrigerate for 30 minutes.

2 **Heat the remaining oil in a large,** heavy-based frying pan and add the fish in batches. Cook for 1 minute on each side. Return all the fish to the pan, then reduce the heat to low and add any remaining marinade and the coconut cream. Season with salt and gently cook for 3–5 minutes, or until the fish is cooked through and flakes easily. If the sauce is too runny, lift out the fish, simmer the sauce for a few minutes, then pour it over the fish. Garnish with the coriander leaves.

PRAWNS WITH GREEN MANGO

SERVES 4

250 g (9 oz) tiger prawns (shrimp)

1½ teaspoons chilli powder

1 teaspoon ground turmeric

½ teaspoon cumin seeds

½ teaspoon yellow mustard seeds

4 garlic cloves, roughly chopped

4 cm (1½ inch) piece of ginger, roughly chopped

1 red onion, roughly chopped

4 tablespoons oil

1 red onion, thinly sliced

1 green unripe mango, finely chopped

1 Peel and devein the prawns, leaving the tails intact. Put the chilli powder, turmeric, cumin, mustard, garlic, ginger and chopped red onion in a blender, food processor or pestle and mortar and process to form a paste. If necessary, add a little water.

2 Heat the oil in a karhai or heavy-based frying pan and fry the sliced onion. When it starts to brown, add the curry paste and fry until aromatic.

3 Add the prawns and 185 ml (6 fl oz/¾ cup) water to the pan, cover and simmer for about 3–4 minutes, until the prawns are cooked and start to curl up. Add the mango and cook for another minute or two to thicken the curry. Season with salt.

ROHU KALIA

SERVES 4

850 g (1 lb 14 oz) skinless rohu, salmon, halibut or cod fillets

4–6 tablespoons mustard oil

5 cm (2 inch) cinnamon stick

5 cardamom pods

4 cloves

4 Indian bay leaves (cassia leaves)

1 onion, finely chopped

4 garlic cloves, crushed

7 cm (2¾ inch) piece of ginger, grated

½ teaspoon ground turmeric

1 teaspoon ground cumin

1 teaspoon chilli powder (optional)

500 ml (17 fl oz/2 cups) thick plain yoghurt

3 green chillies, shredded

1 **Cut the fish into fairly large chunks.** Heat the oil in a karhai or heavy-based frying pan over medium heat and fry the fish a few pieces at a time until golden brown on each side. Drain on paper towels. Add more oil, if necessary, and fry the cinnamon, cardamom, cloves and bay leaves over low heat for 1 minute. Add the onion and fry for 5 minutes, or until golden. Add the garlic, ginger, turmeric, cumin and chilli powder, if using, and fry for 30 seconds.

2 **Remove from the heat** and stir in the yoghurt a little at a time to prevent it curdling. Return to low heat, add the chillies and bring to the boil. Season with salt. Slide in the fish and bring to the boil. Simmer for 10 minutes or until the fish flakes easily and is cooked through. Serve immediately as if you let the dish sit, the fish may give off liquid and make the sauce more runny.

FISH IN YOGHURT SAUCE

SERVES 4

1 kg (2 lb 4 oz) skinless, firm white fish fillets such as halibut or cod

3 tablespoons oil

1 onion, chopped

4 cm (1½ inch) piece of ginger, finely chopped

6 garlic cloves, chopped

1 teaspoon ground cumin

2 teaspoons ground coriander

¼ teaspoon ground turmeric

1 teaspoon garam masala

185 ml (6 fl oz/¾ cup) thick plain yoghurt

4 green chillies, finely chopped

coriander (cilantro) leaves

1   Cut each fish fillet into two pieces and very thoroughly pat them dry.

2   Heat the oil in a heavy-based frying pan over low heat and fry the onion until softened and lightly browned. Add the ginger, garlic and spices and stir for 2 minutes. Add the yoghurt and green chilli and bring to the boil. Season with salt, then cover and simmer for 10 minutes. Slide in the pieces of fish and continue to simmer for 10–12 minutes, until the fish flakes easily and is cooked through. Don't overcook or the fish will give off liquid and the sauce will split.

3   Garnish with coriander leaves and serve immediately. If you let the dish sit, the fish may give off liquid and make the sauce more runny.

FISH IN BANANA LEAF

SERVES 4

4 x 120 g (4¼ oz) pieces hilsa (elish) or blue-eye fillet, skinned

1½ tablespoons lemon juice

½ teaspoon salt

3 tablespoons brown mustard seeds

5 cm (2 inch) piece of ginger, chopped

4 green chillies, chopped

3 teaspoons mustard oil

¼ teaspoon ground turmeric

1 teaspoon chilli powder

4 pieces young banana leaf, or foil, cut into neat pieces big enough to wrap the fish

1 **Wash the fish** and pat dry with paper towels. Mix the lemon juice and salt and rub into the fish.

2 **Grind the mustard seeds to a fine powder** in a spice grinder or pestle and mortar. Put the mustard, ginger, chilli, mustard oil, turmeric and chilli powder in a food processor or pestle and mortar and grind to a smooth paste. Soften the banana leaves by dipping them in very hot water. Wipe dry the pieces as they become pliant.

3 **Smear the fish** with the paste to thoroughly coat. Grease the leaves, or foil, with oil. Place a piece of fish and some marinade in the centre of each and loosely fold into a parcel. Tie with kitchen string and put in a steamer over a saucepan of simmering water. Cover and steam for 10–12 minutes. Open a parcel to check that the fish flakes easily and is cooked. Serve still in the banana leaves.

CURRIED SQUID

SERVES 4

1 kg (2 lb 4 oz) fresh squid

1 teaspoon cumin seeds

1 teaspoon coriander seeds

1 teaspoon chilli powder

½ teaspoon ground turmeric

2 tablespoons oil

1 onion, finely chopped

10 curry leaves

½ teaspoon fenugreek seeds

4 garlic cloves, crushed

7 cm (2¾ inch) piece of ginger, grated

4 tablespoons coconut milk powder mixed with 170 ml (5½ fl oz/⅔ cup) water

3 tablespoons lime juice

1 Pull the squid heads and tentacles out of the bodies, along with any innards, and discard. Peel off the skins. Rinse the bodies, pulling out the clear quills, then cut the bodies into 2.5 cm (1 inch) rings.

2 Place a small frying pan over low heat and dry-roast the cumin until aromatic. Remove, then dry-roast the coriander. Grind both to a fine powder with the chilli and turmeric, using a spice grinder or pestle and mortar. Mix the spices with the squid.

3 Heat the oil in a karhai or heavy-based frying pan and fry the onion until lightly browned. Add the curry leaves, fenugreek, garlic, ginger and coconut. Bring slowly to the boil. Add the squid, then stir well. Simmer for 2–3 minutes, or until cooked and tender. Stir in the lime juice, season and serve.

PRAWNS WITH BITTER MELON

SERVES 4

1 kg (2 lb 4 oz) bitter melon, peeled

300 g (10½ oz) tiger prawns (shrimp)

1 tablespoon oil

½ tablespoon ground turmeric

1 tablespoon ground coriander

1 tablespoon ground cumin

1 teaspoon chilli powder

4–5 green chillies

pinch of sugar

1 tablespoon ghee

4 curry leaves

¼ teaspoon cumin seeds

chopped coriander (cilantro) leaves (optional)

1 **Slice the bitter melon** in half and scoop out any seeds and membrane. Slice into half-moon shapes 5 mm (¼ inch) thick. Sprinkle with salt and degorge in a colander for 30 minutes. Rinse and drain, then dry in a tea towel. Peel and devein the prawns.

2 **Heat the oil** in a heavy-based frying pan, add the bitter melon, stir once or twice, then cover and cook for 3–4 minutes. The bitter melon will continue to sweat out liquid. Mix the turmeric, coriander, cumin and chilli powder to a paste with a small amount of water. Add to the pan and cook over high heat until liquid is reduced to almost dry. Add the prawns and green chillies and cook, tossing until dry. Season with the sugar and a little salt.

3 **For the final seasoning** (tarka), heat the ghee in a small pan, fry the curry leaves and cumin for 1 minute, then pour onto the bitter melon and stir in the coriander, if using.

PRAWN CURRY WITH TAMARIND

SERVES 4

500 g (1 lb 2 oz) tiger prawns (shrimp)

½ teaspoon fennel seeds

1 tablespoon oil

2 cinnamon sticks

3 cardamom pods

1 large onion, finely chopped

5 garlic cloves, crushed

2 cm (¾ inch) piece of ginger, grated

1 stalk of curry leaves

1 teaspoon turmeric

1 teaspoon chilli powder

1½ tablespoons tamarind purée

1 **Peel and devein the prawns,** leaving the tails intact. Place a small frying pan over low heat and dry-roast the fennel seeds until aromatic.

2 **Heat the oil in a karhai or heavy-based frying pan** and fry the fennel seeds, cinnamon, cardamom and onion until the onion is brown. Stir in the garlic, ginger and curry leaves, then add the prawns, turmeric, chilli powder and tamarind. Toss over high heat until the prawn tails turn pink and the prawns are cooked through. Remove from the heat and season with salt, to taste.

SALMON CURRY

SERVES 6

SPICE MIX

6 dried chillies

1 tablespoon cumin seeds

1 teaspoon coriander seeds

1 teaspoon mustard seeds

¼ teaspoon garam masala

½ teaspoon ground turmeric

3 tablespoons oil

1 onion, finely sliced

1 ripe tomato, chopped

2 onions, finely chopped

8 garlic cloves, chopped

6 green chillies, chopped

5 cm (2 inch) piece of ginger, grated

125 ml (4 fl oz/½ cup) tamarind purée

3 tablespoons coconut milk powder or coconut cream

1 kg (2 lb 4 oz) salmon cutlets

1 Prepare the spice mix by grinding the chillies, cumin, coriander and mustard seeds to a fine powder using a spice grinder or pestle and mortar, then mixing with the garam masala and turmeric.

2 Heat the oil over low heat in a heavy-based frying pan large enough to hold the pieces of fish in a single layer. Add the sliced onion and fry until golden. Add the tomato, chopped onion, garlic, green chilli and ginger and fry, stirring occasionally, for 20 minutes, or until the oil separates from the sauce.

3 Add the spice mix and the tamarind to the pan and bring to the boil. Add the coconut milk powder or coconut cream and stir until well mixed. Season with salt, to taste. Add the fish and bring slowly to the boil. The sauce is not very liquid but it needs to be made very hot in order to cook the fish. Simmer for 5 minutes, then turn the pieces of fish over and simmer for another 5 minutes, or until the fish is cooked through and the sauce is thick.

TANDOORI LOBSTER

SERVES 4

2 large or 4 small live lobsters

1 egg

4 cm (1½ inch) piece of ginger, grated

½ teaspoon paprika

2 teaspoons soft brown sugar

170 ml (5½ fl oz/⅔ cup) thick (double/heavy) cream

pinch of ajowan

4 garlic cloves, crushed

2 tablespoons lemon juice

2 tablespoons besan flour

2 teaspoons garam masala

½ teaspoon ground white pepper

20 g (¾ oz) unsalted butter, melted, for basting

coriander (cilantro) leaves

1   Place the lobsters in the freezer for 2 hours to immobilize them. Using a large, heavy-bladed knife or cleaver, cut the lobsters in half. Remove the flesh from the tail shells in one piece, then cut the flesh into large chunks. Clean out the head ends of the shells and wash the shells all over, scrubbing out any membrane.

2   Break the egg into a bowl, add the ginger, paprika, sugar, cream, ajowan, garlic, lemon juice, besan flour, garam masala, white pepper and a pinch of salt and whisk together. Brush the lobster pieces with the mixture, then cover and marinate in the fridge for 2 hours.

3   Preheat the oven to its highest setting. Skewer the lobster pieces on long metal skewers, keeping the pieces 2 cm (¾ inch) apart. Put the skewers on a wire rack set over a baking tray.

4   Roast the lobster for 6 minutes, turning once. Baste with the butter and roast again for about 2–4 minutes, until the lobster is cooked through. Roast the shells on a separate tray until they turn red. Take the lobster pieces off the skewers and put them back in the shells, garnish with coriander leaves and serve hot.

FISH WITH KOKUM

SERVES 6

3 x 5 cm (2 inch) pieces kokum or 2 tablespoons tamarind purée

4 ripe tomatoes

2 tablespoons oil

1 teaspoon black mustard seeds

½ teaspoon fenugreek seeds

3 cm (1¼ inch) piece of ginger, grated

4 green chillies, slit in half

1 garlic clove, crushed

2 onions, sliced

1 teaspoon ground turmeric

1 tablespoon ground coriander

250 ml (9 fl oz/1 cup) coconut milk

800 g (1 lb 12 oz) skinless pomfret, sole or leatherjacket fillets, cut into large chunks

1 stalk of curry leaves

1 Rinse the kokum, remove any stones and put the kokum in a bowl with cold water for a few minutes to soften. Meanwhile, score a cross in the top of each tomato. Plunge them into boiling water for 20 seconds, then drain and peel away from the cross. Roughly chop the tomatoes, discarding the cores and seeds and reserving any juices.

2 Remove the kokum from the water and slice it into pieces.

3 Heat the oil over low heat in a karhai or deep, heavy-based frying pan, add the mustard seeds and cook until they start to pop. Add the fenugreek, ginger, chilli, garlic and onion and fry until the onion is soft. Add the turmeric and coriander and fry for 2 minutes. Add the coconut milk, tomato and kokum, bring to the boil and simmer for 5 minutes. Add the fish to the liquid and simmer for 2–3 minutes or until the fish flakes easily and is cooked through. Season with salt, to taste, and add the curry leaves.

BENGALI FRIED FISH

SERVES 4

600 g (1 lb 5 oz) rainbow trout or
    salmon cutlets

1½ tablespoons lemon juice

½ teaspoon ground turmeric

½ teaspoon salt

3 green chillies, chopped

3 ripe tomatoes, chopped

5 cm (2 inch) piece of ginger, chopped

4 tablespoons mustard oil or oil

2 teaspoons panch phoron

½ teaspoon garam masala

1   Sprinkle the fish with the lemon juice and leave for
10 minutes. Wash in cold water and pat dry. Rub the fish
with the combined turmeric and salt.

2   Put the chilli, tomato and ginger in a food processor and
chop until smooth, or finely chop together with a knife.

3   Heat the oil in a heavy-based frying pan over low heat
and fry the fish a few pieces at a time until brown on both
sides. Drain on paper towels. Add more oil if necessary, add
the panch phoron and fry for 1 minute until aromatic. Add the
tomato mixture and fry for another 2 minutes. Add 185 ml
(6 fl oz/¾ cup) water and bring slowly to the boil. Simmer for
3 minutes, add the fish, slowly return to the boil, then simmer
for another 3 minutes. Sprinkle with the garam masala and
season with salt, to taste.

FISH TIKKA

SERVES 6

MARINADE

500 ml (17 fl oz/2 cups) thick plain
    yoghurt

½ onion, finely chopped

2 cm (¾ inch) piece of ginger, grated

4 garlic cloves, crushed

1 teaspoon ground coriander

2 tablespoons lemon juice

1½ tablespoons garam masala

1 teaspoon paprika

1 teaspoon chilli powder

2 tablespoons tomato paste (purée)

1 teaspoon salt

500 g (1 lb 2 oz) skinless firm white fish
    such as halibut, monkfish or blue-eye

2 onions, each cut into 8 chunks

2 small green or red capsicums
    (peppers), each cut into 8 chunks

50 g (1¾ oz) cucumber, peeled and
    diced

1 tablespoon chopped coriander
    (cilantro)

lemon wedges, to serve

1 To make the marinade, mix half the yoghurt with all the other marinade ingredients in a shallow dish that is long enough and deep enough to take the prepared skewers. You will need eight metal skewers.

2 Cut the fish into about 24–32 bite-sized chunks.

3 On each metal skewer, thread three or four pieces of fish and chunks of onion and capsicum, alternating them as you go. Put the skewers in the marinade and turn them so that all the fish and vegetables are well coated. Cover and marinate in the fridge for at least 1 hour, or until you are ready to cook.

4 Preheat the barbecue or grill (broiler). Lift the skewers out of the marinade. Cook on the barbecue, or under a grill on a wire rack set above a baking tray, for 5–6 minutes, turning once, or until the fish is cooked and firm and both the fish and the vegetables are slightly charred.

5 Meanwhile, stir the cucumber and coriander into the other half of the yoghurt. Serve the fish with the yoghurt and lemon wedges.

POULTRY & MEAT

CHICKEN TIKKA

SERVES 4

MARINADE

½ tablespoon paprika

1 teaspoon chilli powder

2 tablespoons garam masala

¼ teaspoon tandoori food colouring

1½ tablespoons lemon juice

4 garlic cloves, roughly chopped

5 cm (2 inch) piece of ginger, roughly chopped

15 g (½ oz) coriander (cilantro) leaves, chopped

125 ml (4 fl oz/½ cup) thick plain yoghurt

500 g (1 lb 2 oz) skinless chicken breast fillets, cut into cubes

lemon wedges, to serve

1 **For the marinade,** blend all the ingredients together in a food processor until smooth, or chop the garlic, ginger and coriander leaves more finely and mix with the rest of the marinade ingredients. Season with salt, to taste.

2 **Put the chicken cubes** in a bowl with the marinade and mix thoroughly. Cover and marinate overnight in the fridge.

3 **Heat the oven** to 200°C (400°F/Gas 6). Thread the chicken pieces onto four metal skewers and put them on a metal rack above a baking tray. Roast, uncovered, for 15–20 minutes, or until the chicken is cooked through and browned around the edges. Serve with wedges of lemon to squeeze over the chicken.

TANDOORI CHICKEN

SERVES 6

1.5 kg (3 lb 5 oz) chicken or skinless
  chicken thighs and drumsticks

MARINADE
2 teaspoons coriander seeds

1 teaspoon cumin seeds

1 onion, roughly chopped

3 garlic cloves, roughly chopped

5 cm (2 inch) piece of ginger,
  roughly chopped

250 ml thick natural yoghurt

grated rind of 1 lemon

3 tablespoons lemon juice

2 tablespoons clear vinegar

1 teaspoon paprika

2 teaspoons garam masala

½ teaspoon tandoori food colouring
  (optional)

2 tablespoons ghee

lemon wedges, to serve

1 **Remove the skin** from the chicken and cut the chicken in half. Using a sharp knife, make 2.5 cm (1 inch) long diagonal incisions on each limb and breast, taking care not to cut through to the bone. If using thighs and drumsticks, trim away any excess fat and make an incision in each piece.

2 **To make the marinade,** place a frying pan over low heat and dry-roast the coriander seeds until aromatic. Remove and dry-roast the cumin seeds. Grind the roasted seeds to a fine powder using a spice grinder or pestle and mortar. In a food processor, blend all the marinade ingredients to form a smooth paste. Season with salt, to taste.

3 **Marinate the chicken** in the spicy yoghurt marinade for at least 8 hours, or overnight. Turn the chicken occasionally in the marinade to ensure that all sides are soaked.

4 **Heat the oven** to 200°C (400°F/Gas 6). Place the chicken on a wire rack on a baking tray. Cover with foil and roast on the top shelf for about 45–50 minutes or until cooked through (test by inserting a skewer into a thigh—the juices should run clear). Baste the chicken with the marinade once during cooking. Remove the foil 15 minutes before the end of cooking, to brown the tandoori mixture. Preheat the grill to its highest setting.

5 **Prior to serving,** while the chicken is still on the rack, heat the ghee, pour it over the chicken halves and cook under the grill for 5 minutes to blacken the edges of the chicken like a tandoor. Serve the chicken with lemon wedges.

MURGH MASALA

SERVES 4

1.5 kg (3 lb 5 oz) skinless chicken thighs or chicken pieces

2 teaspoons ground cumin

2 teaspoons ground coriander

1½ teaspoons garam masala

¼ teaspoon ground turmeric

2 onions, finely chopped

4 garlic cloves, roughly chopped

5 cm (2 inch) piece of ginger, roughly chopped

2 very ripe tomatoes, chopped

3 tablespoons oil or ghee

5 cloves

8 cardamom pods

5 cm (2 inch) cinnamon stick

10 curry leaves

170 ml (5½ fl oz/⅔ cup) thick plain yoghurt

1 **Trim off any excess fat** or skin from the chicken. Mix the cumin, coriander, garam masala and turmeric together and rub it into the chicken.

2 **Put half the onion** with the garlic, ginger and chopped tomato in a food processor and blend to a smooth paste. If you don't have a blender, finely chop the ingredients and mix them together.

3 **Heat the oil** or ghee in a karhai or casserole over low heat, add the remaining onion, the cloves, cardamom, cinnamon and curry leaves and fry until the onion is golden brown. Add the tomato and onion paste and stir for 5 minutes. Season with salt, to taste. Add the spiced chicken, stir in the yoghurt and bring slowly to the boil.

4 **Reduce the heat,** cover and simmer for 50 minutes or until the oil separates from the sauce. Stir the ingredients occasionally to prevent the chicken from sticking. If the sauce is too thin, simmer for a couple of minutes with the lid off. Season with salt, to taste.

QUAIL MASALA

SERVES 6

6 x 150 g (5½ oz) quails

MARINADE

100 g (3½ oz/⅔ cup) blanched almonds

3 garlic cloves, crushed

3 cm (1¼ inch) piece of ginger, grated

½ onion, finely chopped

½ teaspoon chilli powder

½ teaspoon ground cloves

½ teaspoon ground cinnamon

1 teaspoon ground cumin

1 teaspoon garam masala

2 tablespoons mint leaves, finely chopped

185 ml (6 fl oz/¾ cup) thick plain yoghurt

1 teaspoon jaggery or soft brown sugar

RICE STUFFING

60 g (2¼ oz/¼ cup) rice

1 teaspoon amchoor powder

50 g (1¾ oz) chopped pine nuts

1½ tablespoons lemon juice

2 young banana leaves

3 tablespoons lemon juice

cucumber slices, mango or green mango slices and mint leaves, to serve

1   Clean the quails by rinsing them well and wiping them dry. Prick the flesh all over.

2   To make the marinade, grind the almonds in a food processor or finely chop them with a knife, then mix them with the remaining marinade ingredients. Coat the quails evenly with the marinade, then cover and marinate for 4 hours, or overnight, in the fridge.

3   To make the rice stuffing, preheat the oven to 200°C (400°F/Gas 6). Cook the rice in boiling water for 15 minutes or until just tender. Drain well and allow to cool. Combine the rice, amchoor powder, pine nuts and lemon juice and season with salt. Just before cooking, fill the quails with the rice stuffing and brush some marinade on the quails.

4   If you are making the stuffing in advance, make sure you refrigerate it until you are ready to use it.

5   Cut the banana leaves into neat pieces big enough to wrap a quail. Soften the leaves by dipping them into a pan of very hot water. Wipe them dry as they become pliant. If you can't get banana leaves, use foil. Brush with oil.

6   Wrap each quail individually in a piece of banana leaf, drizzling with any excess marinade. Tie firmly with a piece of kitchen string. Place the parcels, with the seam side up, on a rack above a baking tray and bake for 25–30 minutes. Check to see if the quails are cooked by opening one—the flesh should be slightly pink but the juices should run clear when the flesh is pierced. If necessary, cook the quails for another 5 minutes. Open the packets completely for 3 minutes at the end of cooking, to brown the quail slightly. Sprinkle a dash of lemon juice over each quail. Serve in the packets with some sliced cucumber, sliced mango and mint leaves.

KASHMIRI CHICKEN

SERVES 4

1.5 kg (3 lb 5 oz) chicken or chicken pieces

6 cardamom pods

½ teaspoon coriander seeds

½ teaspoon cumin seeds

2 cm (¾ inch) cinnamon stick

8 peppercorns

6 cloves

100 g (3½ oz/⅔ cup) blanched almonds

75 g (2½ oz/½ cup) shelled pistachios

2 tablespoons ghee or oil

1 onion, finely chopped

4 garlic cloves, finely chopped

5 cm (2 inch) piece of ginger, finely chopped

125 ml (4 fl oz/½ cup) chicken stock

250 ml (9 fl oz/1 cup) thick plain yoghurt

½ teaspoon saffron threads

1 This chicken dish, combining nuts and saffron, is delicately flavoured with a creamy sauce. to make the spices more aromatic, It is best to dry-roast them as suggested in the recipe, rather than use ready-ground ones.

2 If using a whole chicken, cut it into eight pieces by removing both legs and cutting between the joint of the drumstick and thigh. Cut down either side of the backbone and remove the backbone. Turn the chicken over and cut through the cartilage down the centre of the breastbone. Remove the skin from the chicken and cut the flesh off the bones. Cut the chicken into bite-sized pieces. (You can reserve the carcass for making stock if you wish.)

3 Remove the seeds from the cardamom pods. Place a small frying pan over low heat and dry-roast the coriander seeds until aromatic. Remove and dry-roast the cumin seeds, then the piece of cinnamon stick. Grind the cardamom seeds, roasted spices, peppercorns and cloves to a fine powder using a spice grinder or pestle and mortar. Finely chop the almonds and pistachios in a food processor or spice grinder, or with a knife.

4 Heat the ghee or oil in a karhai or casserole over low heat and fry the onion until golden brown. Add the garlic, ginger and chicken and fry rapidly for about 5 minutes. Add the ground spices and the chicken stock and simmer, covered tightly for 30 minutes.

5 Stir the ground nuts into the yoghurt. Mix the saffron with 1 teaspoon of hot water. Add the yoghurt and the saffron to the pan and bring to the boil. Simmer, uncovered, for 10 minutes. Season with salt, to taste.

BUTTER CHICKEN

SERVES 6

2 cm (¾ inch) piece of ginger, roughly chopped

3 garlic cloves, roughly chopped

80 g (2¾ oz/½ cup)blanched almonds

170 ml (5½ fl oz/⅔ cup) thick natural yoghurt

½ teaspoon chilli powder

¼ teaspoon ground cloves

¼ teaspoon ground cinnamon

1 teaspoon garam masala

4 cardamom pods, lightly crushed

400 g (14 oz) tinned chopped tomatoes

1¼ teaspoons salt

1 kg (2 lb 4 oz) chicken skinless, boneless thigh fillets, cut into fairly large pieces

5 tablespoons ghee or clarified butter

1 large onion, thinly sliced

6 tablespoons finely chopped coriander (cilantro) leaves

4 tablespoons thick (double/heavy) cream

1 **Blend the ginger and garlic together** to a paste in a food processor or pestle and mortar, or crush the garlic and finely grate the ginger and mix them together. Grind the almonds in a food processor or finely chop with a knife. Put the paste and almonds in a bowl with the yoghurt, chilli powder, cloves, cinnamon, garam masala, cardamom pods, tomato and salt, and blend together with a fork. Add the chicken pieces and stir to coat thoroughly. Cover and marinate for 2 hours, or overnight, in the fridge.

2 **Preheat the oven** to 180°C (350°F/Gas 4). Heat the ghee or clarified butter in a karhai or deep, heavy-based frying pan, add the onion and fry until softened and brown. Add the chicken mixture and fry for 2 minutes. Mix in the fresh coriander. Put the mixture into a shallow baking dish, pour in the cream and stir with a fork.

3 **Bake for 1 hour.** If the top is browning too quickly during cooking, cover with a piece of foil. Leave to rest for 10 minutes before serving. The oil will rise to the surface. Just before serving, place the dish under a hot grill for about 2 minutes to brown the top. Before serving, slightly tip the dish and spoon off any extra oil.

PARSI CHICKEN WITH APRICOTS

SERVES 4

1.5 kg (3 lb 5 oz) whole chicken or chicken pieces

3 tablespoons oil

2 large onions, finely sliced

1 garlic clove, finely chopped

4 cm (1½ inch) piece of ginger, finely chopped

3 dried chillies

1½ teaspoons garam masala

2 tablespoons tomato paste (concentrated purée)

1 teaspoon salt

2 tablespoons clear vinegar

1½ tablespoons jaggery or soft brown sugar

12 dried apricots

POTATO STRAWS

1 large waxy potato

1 tablespoon salt

oil, for deep-frying

1 **If using a whole chicken,** cut it into eight pieces by removing both legs and cutting between the joint of the drumstick and thigh. Cut down either side of the backbone and remove the backbone. Turn the chicken over and cut through the cartilage down the centre of the breastbone. Cut each breast in half, leaving the wing attached to the top half. Trim off the wing tips.

2 **Heat the oil** in a karhai or casserole. Add the onion and stir over medium heat until softened and starting to brown. Stir in the garlic, ginger, dried chillies and garam masala, then add the chicken. Stir and brown the chicken for 5 minutes. Add the tomato paste, salt and 250 ml (9 fl oz/1 cup) water. Bring to the boil, then reduce the heat, cover and simmer for 20 minutes.

3 **Add the vinegar,** jaggery and dried apricots to the pan, cover and simmer for another 15 minutes.

4 **To make** the potato straws, grate the potato on the largest holes of a grater, then put in a large bowl with about 1.5 litres (52 fl oz/6 cups) water and the salt. Stir and remove some potato a handful at a time, squeezing and patting it dry on a tea towel. Fill a karhai or deep, heavy-based saucepan one-third full with oil. Heat the oil slowly to 160°C/315°F (a cube of bread will brown in 30 seconds), then add a small handful of potato. Be careful not to add too much as it will make the oil bubble and rise up the pan at first. When the potato is golden and crisp, remove it and drain on paper towels. Cook all the potato in the same way.

5 **Serve the chicken pieces** garnished with the potato straws.

SPICY ROAST CHICKEN IN BANANA LEAVES

SERVES 6

2 kg (4 lb 8 oz) chicken

3 tablespoons lemon juice

1 tablespoon oil

2 large onions, roughly chopped

4 garlic cloves, crushed

4 cm (1½ inch) piece of ginger, roughly chopped

3 tablespoons ground almonds

½ teaspoon chilli powder

1 teaspoon ground turmeric

2 teaspoons garam masala

3 coriander (cilantro) roots, chopped

4 tablespoons chopped coriander (cilantro) leaves

3–4 young banana leaves

1 Trim off any excess fat from the chicken. Pat the chicken completely dry with paper towels and prick all over with a skewer so the marinade can penetrate the flesh. Rub the lemon juice and 1 teaspoon of salt all over the skin and inside the cavity of the chicken.

2 Heat the oil in a heavy-based frying pan over low heat, add the onion and cook until the onion starts to brown. Add the garlic and ginger and cook for 2 minutes, or until soft. Add the almonds, chilli powder, turmeric and garam masala and cook for 1 minute. Allow the onion mixture to cool completely.

3 Place the cooled mixture in a food processor or a pestle and mortar, along with the coriander roots and leaves. Grind to a smooth paste and rub the paste thoroughly all over the chicken and inside the cavity. Cover and refrigerate for 6 hours or overnight.

4 Preheat the oven to 200°C (400°F/Gas 6). Soften the banana leaves by dipping them into a pan of very hot water. Wipe the pieces dry as they become pliant. Tie the legs of the chicken together to keep them in place.

5 Wrap the chicken in the banana leaves, making sure that it is well covered. Tie a piece of kitchen string around the chicken like a parcel. If you can't buy banana leaves, wrap the chicken in a large sheet of foil instead. Place the chicken in a roasting tin and bake for 1½ hours. Unwrap the banana leaves or the foil from around the top of the chicken, baste the chicken with some of the juices and return it to the oven for 10 minutes, or until well browned. Check that the chicken is cooked by pulling away one leg—the juices should run clear. Rest the chicken for 10 minutes before carving.

MOGHUL-STYLE LAMB

SERVES 4

6 garlic cloves, roughly chopped

4 cm (1½ inch) piece of ginger, roughly chopped

50 g (2 oz/⅓ cup) blanched almonds

2 onions, thinly sliced

750 g (1 lb 10 oz) boneless leg or shoulder of lamb, cut into 2.5 cm (1 inch) cubes

2 teaspoons coriander seeds

40 g (1½ oz) ghee

7 cardamom pods

5 cloves

1 cinnamon stick

1 teaspoon salt

310 ml (10¾ fl oz/1¼ cups) cream

½ teaspoon cayenne pepper

½ teaspoon garam masala

flaked toasted almonds, to garnish

1   Blend the garlic, ginger, almonds and 50 g (1¾ oz) of the onion in a blender or food processor. If you don't have a blender, finely chop them with a knife or grind together in a pestle and mortar. Add a little water if necessary to make a smooth paste, then put in a bowl with the lamb and mix thoroughly to coat the meat. Cover and marinate in the fridge for 2 hours, or overnight.

2   Place a small frying pan over low heat, dry-roast the coriander seeds until aromatic, then grind to a fine powder using a spice grinder or pestle and mortar.

3   Heat the ghee in a karhai or casserole. Add the cardamom pods, cloves and cinnamon stick and, after a few seconds, add the remaining onion and fry until it is soft and starting to brown. Transfer the onion to a plate.

4   Fry the meat and the marinade in the pan until the mixture is quite dry and has started to brown a little. Add 170 ml (5½ fl oz/⅔ cup) hot water to the pan, cover tightly and cook over low heat for 30 minutes, stirring occasionally.

5   Add the ground coriander, salt, cream, cayenne pepper and cooked onion to the pan, cover and simmer for another 30 minutes, or until the lamb is tender. Stir occasionally to prevent the lamb from sticking to the pan. Remove the cardamom pods, cloves and cinnamon stick, then stir in the garam masala. Sprinkle with flaked almonds.

DHANSAK

SERVES 6

100 g (3½ oz) toor dal (yellow lentils)

25 g (1 oz) moong dal

25 g (1 oz) chickpeas

50 g (1¾ oz) masoor dal (red lentils)

1 eggplant (aubergine), unpeeled

150 g (5½ oz) pumpkin, unpeeled

150 g (5½ oz) amaranth or English spinach leaves

2 tomatoes

2 green chillies

2 tablespoons ghee or oil

1 onion, finely chopped

3 garlic cloves, crushed

2 cm (¾ inch) piece of ginger, grated

1 kg (2 lb 4 oz) boneless leg or shoulder of lamb, cut into 3 cm (1¼ inch) cubes

2 cm (¾ inch) cinnamon stick

5 cardamom pods, bruised

3 cloves

1 tablesoon ground coriander

1 teaspoon ground turmeric

1 teaspoon chilli powder, or to taste

3 tablespoons lime juice

1 Soak the toor dal, moong dal and chickpeas in plenty of water for about 2 hours. Drain well.

2 Put all four types of pulse in a saucepan, add about 1 litre (35 fl oz/4 cups) of water, cover and bring to the boil. Uncover and simmer for 15 minutes, skimming off any scum that forms on the surface, and stirring occasionally to make sure all the pulses are cooking at the same rate and are soft. Lightly mash the soft pulses to a similar texture.

3 Cook the eggplant and pumpkin in boiling water for 10–15 minutes, or until soft. Scoop out the pumpkin flesh and cut it into pieces. Peel the eggplant carefully (it may be very pulpy) and cut it into small pieces. Cut the amaranth or spinach into 5 cm (2 inch) lengths, halve the tomatoes and split the chillies lengthwise, removing any seeds.

4 Heat the ghee or oil in a karhai or casserole and fry the onion, garlic and ginger for 5 minutes, or until lightly brown and softened. Add the lamb and brown for about 10 minutes, or until aromatic. Add the cinnamon, cardamom pods, cloves, coriander, turmeric and chilli powder and fry for 5 minutes to allow the flavours to develop. Add 170 ml (5½ fl oz/⅔ cup) water, cover and simmer for 40 minutes, or until the lamb is tender.

5 Add the mashed lentils and all the cooked and raw vegetables to the pan. Season with the lime juice and salt and pepper. Simmer for 15 minutes (if the sauce is too thick, add a little water). Stir well, then check the seasoning. The dhansak should be flavoursome, aromatic, tart and spicy.

ALOO GOSHT

SERVES 6

1.5 kg (3 lb 5 oz) leg of lamb on the bone

350 g (12 oz) waxy potatoes

1½ teaspoons coriander seeds

1½ teaspoons cumin seeds

2 tablespoons oil

1 onion, chopped

2 Indian bay leaves (cassia leaves)

¼ teaspoon ground turmeric

2 teaspoons garam masala

400 g (14 oz) tinned chopped tomatoes

3 green chillies, chopped

4 garlic cloves, crushed

3 cm (1¼ inch) piece of ginger, grated

1 tablespoon tomato paste (concentrated purée)

1 Trim away any excess fat from the lamb, remove the bone and cut the lamb into 3 cm (1¼ inch) cubes. Reserve the bones with their marrow.

2 Cut each potato into large chunks and put in a bowl of cold water.

3 Place a small frying pan over low heat and dry-roast the coriander seeds until aromatic. Remove them, then dry-roast the cumin seeds. Grind the roasted spices to a fine powder using a spice grinder or pestle and mortar.

4 Heat the oil in a karhai or casserole over low heat. Add the onion and bay leaves and fry over low heat until lightly browned. Stir in the coriander and cumin mixture, turmeric and 1 teaspoon of garam masala. Add the tomato, chilli, garlic and ginger and fry until the oil separates out of the sauce. Stir in the tomato paste, then 250 ml (9 fl oz/1 cup) water. Add the lamb and bone and mix well. Bring to the boil, cover tightly, reduce the heat and simmer for 1 hour.

5 Add the potato chunks to the pan and cook for another hour, occasionally shaking the pan to prevent the meat from sticking. If all the liquid has evaporated, add 125 ml (4 fl oz/ ½ cup) hot water. When the meat is cooked, the sauce should be fairly thick. Season with salt, to taste.

6 Remove the bone before serving. Serve sprinkled with the remaining garam masala.

METHI GOSHT

SERVES 4

2 onions, roughly chopped

4 garlic cloves, roughly chopped

8 cm (3 inch) piece of ginger, roughly chopped

3 green chillies (seed them for less heat)

125 ml (4 fl oz/½ cup) oil

2 Indian bay leaves (cassia leaves)

1 kg (2 lb 4 oz) boneless lamb leg or shoulder, cut into 2.5 cm (1 inch) cubes

1 tablespoon ground cumin

2 tablespoons ground coriander

½ teaspoon garam masala

½ teaspoon chilli powder

2 teaspoons salt

½ teaspoon ground black pepper

4 bunches of fresh methi leaves, finely chopped (about 200 g/7 oz)

1 Blend the onion, garlic, ginger and chillies together in a blender or food processor until finely chopped. If you don't have a blender, finely chop them together with a knife or crush them in a pestle and mortar.

2 Heat the oil in a karhai or large casserole over medium heat and add the chopped mixture and the bay leaves. Cook for 3 minutes, or until golden and just starting to catch on the base of the pan. Add the cubed lamb in batches, stirring for about 20 minutes, until it is all browned. The juices of the meat will start to run clear and the oil will separate out. You need to keep stirring or the meat will catch on the base of the pan.

3 Add all the spices, and the salt and pepper, and fry for 3 minutes, or until all pieces of the lamb are thoroughly coated. Add 185 ml (6 fl oz/¾ cup) water, bring to the boil, then reduce the heat, cover and simmer for 45 minutes, adding a little more water if necessary. The sauce should be dryish rather than sloppy. Gently stir in the methi and cook for another 15 minutes, or until the oil separates from the lamb and the sauce has turned a rich olive green.

LAMB KALIA

SERVES 6

2½ teaspoons cumin seeds

125 ml (4 fl oz/½ cup) thick plain yoghurt

2 teaspoons clear vinegar

1 teaspoon salt

1 tablespoon ginger juice

3 teaspoons chilli powder

1 teaspoon ground turmeric

1 kg (2 lb 4 oz) lamb leg or chump, cut into 2.5 cm (1 inch) cubes

2 potatoes, cut into 2.5 cm (1 inch) cubes

oil for deep-frying

3 cm (1¼ inch) cinnamon stick

2 cardamom pods, crushed

4 garlic cloves, crushed

½ teaspoon sugar

4 onions, sliced

2 Indian bay leaves (cassia leaves)

1 tablespoon tomato paste (concentrated purée)

1 **Place a small frying pan** over low heat and dry-roast 2 teaspoons of the cumin seeds until aromatic. Grind the roasted cumin seeds to a fine powder using a spice grinder or pestle and mortar.

2 **Combine the ground cumin** with the yoghurt, vinegar, salt, ginger juice, chilli powder and ½ teaspoon of the turmeric in a large bowl.

3 **Add the lamb and coat well.** Cover and marinate for at least 2 hours in the fridge.

4 **Coat the potato** with the remaining ½ teaspoon of turmeric. Fill a karhai or casserole one-third full with oil and heat to 180°C/350°F (a cube of bread will brown in 15 seconds). Fry the potato cubes until they are golden brown, then remove and drain on paper towels. Let the oil cool a little, then pour out all but 2 tablespoons.

5 **Place the pan** back over medium heat and fry the remaining cumin seeds until they start to pop. Add the cinnamon stick, cardamom pods, garlic, sugar and onion and fry until golden.

6 **Add the meat** to the pan and fry until the meat is browned (you may need to add a bit more of the oil). Add the bay leaves, tomato paste and 250 ml (1 cup) water and reduce the heat. Cover and simmer for 1 hour, or until the lamb is tender. If the sauce is still a little thin when the lamb is cooked, simmer with the lid off until it thickens. Toss the potato through the meat before serving.

MANGALOREAN PORK BAFATH

SERVES 6

20 red Kashmiri chillies, seeded

2 teaspoons coriander seeds

1 teaspoon cumin seeds

½ teaspoon ground turmeric

10 black peppercorns

2 tablespoons tamarind purée

1.5 kg (3 lb 5 oz) boneless pork leg or shoulder, cut into 3 cm (1¼ inch) cubes

1 tablespoon oil

2 onions, cut into 3 cm (1¼ inch) pieces

2 cm (¾ inch) piece of ginger, finely chopped

6 green chillies, slit lengthwise into halves

8 cloves

2 cm (¾ inch) cinnamon stick, pounded roughly

1 tablespoon dark vinegar

3 garlic cloves, finely chopped

1 green chilli, extra, seeded, finely sliced lengthwise

1 Place a small frying pan over low heat and dry-roast the chillies, coriander seeds, cumin seeds, ground turmeric and peppercorns until aromatic. Grind the roasted mixture to a fine powder using a spice grinder or pestle and mortar.

2 Mix all the roasted, ground ingredients with the tamarind and meat. Cover and marinate in the fridge for 2 hours.

3 Heat the oil in a karhai or casserole over high heat, add the meat mixture in batches and brown all over. Return all the meat to the pan, then add the onion, ginger, chilli, cloves and cinnamon. Stir thoroughly to mix with the pork. Reduce the heat to low and cook for about 20 minutes, until the meat juices appear and mix with the spice, creating a thick sauce.

4 Add the vinegar, garlic and 250 ml (9 fl oz/1 cup) water and cook for 1–1¼ hours, until the pork is very tender. Season with salt, to taste. Cook until the oil separates from the spice mixture, which indicates the meat is ready. You can skim off the oil or blot it from the surface with paper towels if you prefer. Garnish with the chilli before serving.

PORK WITH CAPSICUM AND POTATOES

SERVES 6

125 ml (4 fl oz/½ cup) oil

1 large onion, chopped

4 garlic cloves, crushed

8 cm (3 inch) piece of ginger, chopped

2 Indian bay leaves (cassia leaves)

600 g (1 lb 5 oz) pork sparerib chops, meat cut into 2 cm (¾ inch) cubes

pinch of asafoetida

1 teaspoon chilli powder

½ teaspoon ground turmeric

1½ tablespoons ground cumin

1½ tablespoons ground coriander

½ teaspoon garam masala

1½ tablespoons lemon juice

4 dried chillies

1 teaspoon kalonji (nigella seeds)

1 teaspoon yellow mustard seeds

2 tomatoes, finely chopped

4 green chillies

2 teaspoons paprika

2 red capsicums (peppers), cut into 2.5 cm (1 inch) pieces

2 green capsicums (peppers), cut into 2.5 cm (1 inch) pieces

1 tablespoon salt

1 teaspoon ground black pepper

500 g (1 lb 2 oz) potatoes, cut into 3 cm (1¼ inch) cubes

10 curry leaves

1 Heat **80 ml** (2½ fl oz/⅓ cup) of the oil in a karhai or casserole over medium heat. Add half of each of the onion, garlic and ginger, along with the bay leaves and fry for about 2 minutes, until the onion is soft. Increase the heat to high, add the meat and asafoetida and fry for 2 minutes, stirring until all the meat is brown. Reduce the heat to medium and cook for 10 minutes. Remove from the heat, lift out the meat with a spatula and place in a large bowl.

2 Add **the chilli powder**, turmeric, 1¼ tablespoons cumin, 2 teaspoons coriander and the garam masala to the meat, stirring in while the meat is still warm. Stir in the lemon juice.

3 Heat **the remaining oil** in the same pan over medium heat and fry the remaining onion, garlic and ginger for a few minutes until the onion is soft. Add the dried chillies, kalonji, yellow mustard seeds and the remaining coriander and

cumin. Fry for 2 minutes, or until the seeds start to pop. Add the chopped tomato and fry for 1 minute. Reduce the heat to simmering and cook for 5 minutes, or until the liquid from the tomato has reduced.

4 Stir in **the green chillies** and the paprika. Add the meat and stir over medium heat for 2 minutes, or until all the sauce has been absorbed by the meat. Add the red and green capsicum, then reduce the heat to simmering and cover the pan. Cook for 10 minutes, then add the salt, pepper and cubed potato.

5 Add **125 ml** (4 fl oz/½ cup) water, cover and simmer for 1 hour, stirring occasionally. Add the curry leaves and cook for another 15 minutes. The meat and potato should be very tender, but if not, cook for another 15 minutes. Add 1 teaspoon of extra garam masala and season with salt, to taste.

PORK VINDALOO

SERVES 4

1 kg (2 lb 4 oz) leg of pork on the bone
6 cardamom pods
1 teaspoon black peppercorns
4 dried chillies
1 teaspoon cloves
10 cm (4 inch) cinnamon stick, roughly broken
1 teaspoon cumin seeds
½ teaspoon ground turmeric
½ teaspoon coriander seeds
¼ teaspoon fenugreek seeds
4 tablespoons clear vinegar
1 tablespoon dark vinegar
4 tablespoons oil
2 onions, finely sliced
10 garlic cloves, finely sliced
5 cm (2 inch) piece of ginger, cut into matchsticks
3 ripe tomatoes, roughly chopped
4 green chillies, chopped
1 teaspoon jaggery or soft brown sugar

1　Trim away any excess fat from the pork, remove the bone and cut the pork into 2.5 cm (1 inch) cubes. Reserve the bone.

2　Split open the cardamom pods and remove the seeds. Finely grind the cardamom seeds, peppercorns, dried chillies, cloves, cinnamon stick, cumin seeds, turmeric, coriander seeds and fenugreek seeds in a spice grinder or pestle and mortar.

3　In a large bowl, mix the ground spices together with the vinegars. Add the pork and mix thoroughly to coat well. Cover and marinate in the fridge for 3 hours.

4　Heat the oil in a karhai or casserole over low heat and fry the onion until lightly browned. Add the garlic, ginger, tomato and chilli and stir well. Add the pork, increase the heat to high and fry for 3–5 minutes, or until browned. Add 250 ml (9 fl oz/1 cup) water and any of the marinade liquid left in the bowl, reduce the heat and bring slowly back to the boil. Add the jaggery and the pork bone. Cover tightly and simmer for about 1½ hours, stirring occasionally until the meat is very tender. Discard the bone. Season with salt, to taste.

FRIED BEEF KERALA

SERVES 4

oil for deep-frying

1 potato, cut into small cubes

500 g (1 lb 2 oz) rump steak,
  thinly sliced

3 garlic cloves, crushed

1 teaspoon ground black pepper

1 tablespoon ginger juice

2 tablespoons oil, extra

2 onions, sliced in rings

60 ml (2 fl oz/¼ cup) beef stock

2 tablespoons tomato paste
  (concentrated purée)

½ tablespoon soy sauce

1 teaspoon chilli powder

3 tablespoons lemon juice

3 tomatoes, chopped

80 g (2¾ oz) fresh or frozen peas

coriander (cilantro) leaves (optional)

1 **Fill a deep,** heavy-based saucepan one-third full with oil and heat to 180°C/350°F (a cube of bread will brown in 15 seconds). Deep-fry the potato cubes until golden brown. Drain on paper towels.

2 **Put the steak in a bowl,** add the garlic, pepper and ginger juice and toss well. Heat the oil and fry the beef quickly in batches over high heat. Keep each batch warm as you remove it. Reduce the heat, fry the onion until golden, then remove.

3 **Put the stock,** tomato paste, soy sauce, chilli powder and lemon juice in the pan and cook over medium heat until reduced. Add the fried onion, cook for 3 minutes, add the chopped tomato and the peas, then stir well and cook for 1 minute. Add the beef and potato and toss well until heated through. Garnish with coriander leaves if you like.

LAMB KORMA

SERVES 4

1 kg (2 lb 4 oz) boneless leg or shoulder of lamb, cut into 2.5 cm (1 inch) cubes

2 tablespoons thick natural yoghurt

1 tablespoon coriander seeds

2 teaspoons cumin seeds

5 cardamom pods

2 onions

2 tablespoons grated coconut

1 tablespoon white poppy seeds (khus khus)

3 green chillies, roughly chopped

4 garlic cloves, crushed

5 cm (2 inch) piece of ginger, grated

25 g (1 oz) cashew nuts

6 cloves

¼ teaspoon ground cinnamon

2 tablespoons oil

1 Put the meat in a bowl, add the yoghurt and mix to coat thoroughly.

2 Place a small frying pan over low heat and dry-roast the coriander seeds until aromatic. Remove and dry-roast the cumin seeds. Grind the roasted mixture to a fine powder using a spice grinder or pestle and mortar. Remove the seeds from the cardamom pods and grind them.

3 Roughly chop one onion and finely slice the other. Put just the roughly chopped onion with the ground spices, coconut, poppy seeds, chilli, garlic, ginger, cashew nuts, cloves and cinnamon in a blender, add 170 ml (5½ fl oz/⅔ cup) water and process to a smooth paste. If you don't have a blender, crush everything together in a pestle and mortar, or finely chop with a knife, before adding the water.

4 Heat the oil in a karhai or casserole over medium heat. Add the finely sliced onion and fry until lightly browned. Pour the blended mixture into the pan, season with salt and cook over low heat for 1 minute, or until the liquid evaporates and the sauce thickens. Add the lamb with the yoghurt and slowly bring to the boil. Cover tightly and simmer for 1½ hours, or until the meat is very tender. Stir the meat occasionally to prevent it from sticking to the pan. If the water has evaporated during the cooking time, add another 125 ml (4 fl oz/½ cup) of water to make a sauce. The sauce should be quite thick.

VEGETABLES & PULSES

ALOO GOBI

SERVES 4

3 tablespoons oil

½ teaspoon black mustard seeds

½ onion, finely chopped

200 g (7 oz) potatoes, cut into cubes

¼ teaspoon ground turmeric

1 teaspoon ground cumin

1 teaspoon ground coriander

1½ teaspoons garam masala

4 ripe tomatoes, chopped

1 large cauliflower (about 1.25 kg/
   2 lb 12 oz), cut into florets

2 cm (¾ inch) piece of ginger

1 teaspoon sugar

1 Heat the oil in a karhai or deep, heavy-based frying pan over low heat. Add the mustard seeds, cover the pan and wait for the seeds to pop. Add the onion and potato and fry until lightly browned.

2 Add the turmeric, cumin, coriander and garam masala to the pan and fry for a couple of seconds. Add the tomato and stir until the spices are well mixed.

3 Add the cauliflower florets and stir until well mixed. Stir in the ginger, sugar and 125 ml (4 fl oz/½ cup) water, increase the heat to medium and bring to the boil. Reduce the heat, cover and simmer for 15 minutes, or until the vegetables are tender. Season with salt, to taste.

4 Uncover the pan and if the sauce is too runny, simmer it for another 1–2 minutes before serving.

SNAKE GOURD WITH YOGHURT

SERVES 4

250 g (9 oz) snake gourd

1 teaspoon ground turmeric

1 tablespoon oil

½ teaspoon black mustard seeds

½ teaspoon whole urad dal

2 dried chillies, cut in half

4 stalks of curry leaves

1 large red onion, finely chopped

250 ml (9 fl oz/1 cup) thick plain yoghurt

1 **Peel the snake gourd,** slice in half horizontally and then slice diagonally into pieces about 1 cm (½ inch) thick. Add the turmeric and a pinch of salt and rub into the pieces of gourd. Put the gourd in a sieve to allow any liquid to drain off.

2 **Heat the oil** in a karhai or heavy-based frying pan over low heat. Add the mustard and urad dal and when the mustard seeds pop, add the chilli and curry leaves and one-third of the onion. Cook until the onion is browned and softened. Add the snake gourd and toss over medium heat for about 10 minutes, or until the mixture looks dry and the gourd is tender.

3 **Remove from the heat,** combine the yoghurt and the remaining onion in a bowl and stir well. Fold the fried snake gourd into the yoghurt just before serving and season with salt, to taste.

SPICY EGGPLANT

SERVES 6

800 g (1 lb 12 oz) eggplants
  (aubergines), cut into wedges 5 cm
  (2 inches) long

400 g (14 oz) ripe tomatoes or 400 g
  (14 oz) tinned chopped tomatoes

2.5 cm (1 inch) piece of ginger, grated

6 garlic cloves, crushed

310 ml (10¾ fl oz/1¼ cups) oil

1 teaspoon fennel seeds

½ teaspoon kalonji (nigella seeds)

1 tablespoon ground coriander

¼ teaspoon ground turmeric

½ teaspoon cayenne pepper

1 teaspoon salt

1 **Put the eggplant pieces** in a colander, sprinkle them with salt and leave them for 30 minutes to allow any bitter juices to run out. Rinse, squeeze out any excess water, then pat dry with paper towels.

2 **If using fresh tomatoes,** score a cross in the top of each and plunge into boiling water for 20 seconds. Drain and peel away from the cross. Roughly chop the tomatoes, discarding the cores and seeds and reserving any juices.

3 **Puree the ginger** and garlic with one-third of the tomato in a blender or food processor. If you don't have a blender, finely chop the tomatoes and mix with the ginger and garlic.

4 **Heat 125 ml** (4 fl oz/½ cup) of the oil in a large, deep, heavy-based frying pan and when hot, add as many eggplant pieces as you can fit in a single layer. Cook over medium heat until brown on both sides, then transfer to a sieve over a bowl

so that the excess oil can drain off. Add the remaining oil to the pan as needed and cook the rest of the eggplant in batches.

5 **Reheat the oil** that's left in the pan and add the fennel seeds and kalonji. Cover and allow to pop for a few seconds. Add the tomato and ginger mixture and the remaining ingredients, except the eggplant. Cook, stirring regularly for 5–6 minutes, until the mixture becomes thick and fairly smooth (be careful as it may spit at you). Carefully add the cooked eggplant so the pieces stay whole, cover the pan and cook gently for about
10 minutes.

6 **Store the eggplant** in the sauce in the fridge. Pour off any excess oil before serving. The eggplant can either be served cold or gently warmed through.

BHINDI MASALA

SERVES 4

500 g (1 lb 2 oz) okra, about
  5 cm (2 inches) long

3 green chillies

3 tablespoons oil

1 teaspoon black mustard seeds

1 red onion, finely chopped

1 teaspoon ground cumin

1 teaspoon ground coriander

2 teaspoons garam masala

1 teaspoon ground turmeric

4 garlic cloves, finely chopped

1 Wash the okra and pat dry with paper towels. Trim the tops and tails. Ignore any sticky, glutinous liquid that appears because this will disappear as the okra cooks.

2 Cut the chillies in half lengthwise, leaving them attached at the stalk, and scrape out any seeds. Heat the oil in a karhai or deep, heavy-based frying pan, add the mustard seeds and onion and cook until the seeds pop and the onion is light brown. Add the cumin, coriander, garam masala and turmeric and cook until the popping stops.

3 Add the garlic, okra and the chilli to the pan, fry for 5 minutes, stir and cook for 2 minutes. Add 60 ml (2 fl oz/ ¼ cup) water, 1 tablespoon at a time, and stir to make a sauce. Season with salt, to taste. Simmer for about 15 minutes, until the okra is cooked through and the sauce is thick and dry.

BHINDI BHAJI

SERVES 4

450 g (1 lb) okra

2 tablespoons oil

1 small onion, finely chopped

½ teaspoon ground cumin

½ teaspoon ground coriander

½ teaspoon chilli powder (optional)

¼ teaspoon ground turmeric

150 g (5½ oz) tinned chopped tomatoes

1 **Wash the okra** and pat dry with paper towels. Trim the ends and cut into 2.5 cm (1 inch) pieces. Ignore any sticky, glutinous liquid that appears because this will disappear as the okra cooks.

2 **Heat the oil** in a karhai or deep, heavy-based frying pan over medium heat and fry the onion until lightly browned. Add the spices and tomato and fry for 1 minute until well mixed, squashing the tomato to break it up.

3 **Add the okra** and stir until well coated. Bring to the boil, cover and simmer for 5–8 minutes, until the okra is cooked through and no longer slimy. If there is any excess liquid, simmer, uncovered, until the liquid evaporates. Season with salt, to taste.

STUFFED CAPSICUMS

SERVES 6

400 g (14 oz) potatoes, quartered

6 small green capsicums (peppers)

2 tablespoons oil

2 onions, finely chopped

2 teaspoons ground cumin

2 teaspoons ground coriander

½ teaspoon ground turmeric

½ teaspoon chilli powder

SAUCE

½ onion, finely chopped

6 cloves

6 cardamom pods

2 garlic cloves, finely chopped

2 cm (¾ inch) piece of ginger, finely chopped

1 cinnamon stick

1 teaspoon ground coriander

1 teaspoon ground cumin

¼ teaspoon ground turmeric

½ teaspoon chilli powder

50 g (1¾ oz) creamed coconut, mixed with 250 ml (9 fl oz/1 cup) water, or 250 ml (9 fl oz/1 cup) coconut cream

1 Cook the potato in a saucepan of simmering water for 15 minutes, or until tender, then drain and cut into small cubes. Bring a large saucepan of water to the boil, add the capsicums and blanch for 5 minutes. Refresh the capsicums in cold water, cut round the stem and remove both it and the seeds. Drain well upside-down.

2 Heat the oil in a small frying pan and cook the onion over medium heat until soft but not browned. Add the cumin, coriander, turmeric and chilli and mix thoroughly. Mix in the potato and season with salt. Remove from the heat and leave until cool. Divide into six portions and fill each capsicum.

3 To make the sauce, combine all the ingredients in a deep, heavy-based frying pan and bring slowly to the boil. Reduce the heat to low, cover and simmer for 20 minutes. Season with salt, to taste. Add the stuffed capsicums to the pan, arranging them so that they stand upright in a single layer, and cook for another 5 minutes, or until the sauce is thick. Serve the capsicums with a little sauce spooned over the top.

SHEBU BHAJI

SERVES 2

200 g (7 oz) potatoes

200 g (7 oz) dill

2 tablespoons oil

2 garlic cloves, chopped

¼ teaspoon ground turmeric

1 teaspoon black mustard seeds

pinch of asafoetida

1 dried chilli

1 Cut the potatoes into 2.5 cm (1 inch) cubes and cook in a saucepan of simmering water for 15 minutes or until just tender. Drain well.

2 Wash the dill in several changes of water and trim off the tough stalks. Roughly chop the dill.

3 Heat the oil in a heavy-based saucepan, add the garlic and fry for 30 seconds over low heat. Add the turmeric, mustard seeds, asafoetida and the whole chilli, cover and briefly allow the seeds to pop. Stir in the potato until well mixed. Add the dill, cover and cook over low heat for 5 minutes. The dill contains sufficient moisture to cook without the addition of any water. Season with salt, to taste.

MOOLI BHAJI

SERVES 4

500 g (1 lb 2 oz) mooli

25 g (1 oz) grated coconut

2 tablespoons oil

¼ teaspoon black mustard seeds

1 onion, chopped

¼ teaspoon ground turmeric

pinch of asafoetida

1 green chilli, finely chopped

1 Cut the mooli into batons. Heat a frying pan over low heat and dry-roast the coconut, stirring constantly until it browns lightly.

2 Heat the oil in a karhai or heavy-based saucepan over low heat. Add the mustard seeds, cover and allow to pop briefly. Add the onion and cook until lightly browned. Stir in the turmeric, asafoetida, chilli and the mooli until well mixed. Add 125 ml (4 fl oz/½ cup) water and simmer for 5–7 minutes, until the mooli is cooked through and tender. Season with salt, to taste. Garnish with the coconut.

SPICED BANANA FLOWER

SERVES 4

1 banana flower

½ lemon

200 g (7 oz) prawns (shrimp)

25 g (1 oz) grated coconut

1 tablespoon oil

125 ml (4 fl oz/½ cup) lime juice

1 red chilli, finely chopped

2 tablespoons jaggery or
   soft brown sugar

1 tablespoon grated lime zest,
   or lime leaves

mint leaves

1 **Peel off one leaf at a time** from the banana flower. Remove the yellow, stick-like immature bananas and discard both them and the leaves until you reach the white inner core. Chop off the top end and discard it. Chop what is left into quarters and soak it in a bowl of water with 1 teaspoon salt for 1 hour. Drain the banana flower, transfer to a saucepan, cover with fresh water and add the juice from the half lemon. Bring to the boil and cook for 15–20 minutes, or until soft. The banana flower will darken in colour as it cooks. Drain and slice into julienne strips. Peel and devein the prawns and cut each in half.

2 **Place a heavy-based frying pan** over low heat and dry-roast the coconut, stirring constantly until the coconut is golden brown. Finely grind in a pestle and mortar or in a spice grinder.

3 **Heat the oil** in the frying pan and fry the prawns until they are pink and cooked through. Mix the prawns with the lime juice, chilli, jaggery and lime rind. Season with salt, to taste, then leave to cool.

4 **Just before serving,** add the banana hearts and coconut to the prawns and toss well. Serve cold, garnished with the mint leaves.

CABBAGE WITH SPLIT PEAS

SERVES 4

125 g (4½ oz) split peas

450 g (1 lb) green cabbage

3 tablespoons oil

¼ teaspoon black mustard seeds

2 teaspoons cumin seeds

8 curry leaves

2 dried chillies

pinch of asafoetida

¼ teaspoon ground turmeric

coriander (cilantro) leaves (optional)

1 Soak the split peas in 750 ml (26 fl oz/3 cups) boiling water for 2 hours. Drain thoroughly.

2 Shred the cabbage.

3 Heat the oil in a karhai or deep, heavy-based frying pan over low heat.

4 Add the mustard and cumin seeds, cover and allow to pop briefly. Add the curry leaves, dried chillies and split peas and fry for 5 minutes, stirring often.

5 Add the asafoetida, turmeric and cabbage and fry over low heat until the cabbage is cooked through and tender. Season with salt, to taste.

6 Serve garnished with coriander leaves if you wish.

PUNJABI CABBAGE

SERVES 4

½ onion, roughly chopped

1 garlic clove, roughly chopped

2.5 cm (1 inch) piece of ginger, chopped

2 green chillies, seeded and chopped

4 tablespoons oil

1 teaspoon cumin seeds

1 teaspoon ground turmeric

500 g (1 lb 2 oz) green cabbage, finely shredded

1 teaspoon salt

½ teaspoon ground black pepper

2 teaspoons ground cumin

1 teaspoon ground coriander

¼ teaspoon chilli powder

1 tablespoon unsalted butter

1 Put the onion, garlic, ginger and chilli in a food processor and chop until finely chopped but not a paste, or chop together with a knife.

2 Heat the oil in a karhai or heavy-based frying pan over low heat and fry the onion mixture until softened but not browned. Add the cumin seeds and turmeric to the pan and stir for 1 minute.

3 Mix in the cabbage, stirring thoroughly until all the leaves are coated in the yellow paste. Add the salt, pepper, ground cumin, coriander and chilli powder. Stir to coat the cabbage, then cook for 10 minutes with the pan partially covered, stirring occasionally until the cabbage is soft. If the cabbage becomes too dry and starts sticking to the pan, add 1–2 tablespoons water. Stir in the butter and season with salt, to taste.

MATAR PANEER

SERVES 4

225 g (8 oz) paneer	
2 tablespoons ghee	
50 g (1¾ oz) onion, chopped	
200 g (1⅓ cups) peas	
½ teaspoon sugar	
5 cm (2 inch) piece of ginger, grated	
2–3 green chillies, finely chopped	
1 spring onion (scallion), finely chopped	
½ teaspoon garam masala	
1 tablespoon chopped coriander (cilantro) leaves	

1 **Cut the paneer** into 2 cm (¾ inch) cubes. Heat the ghee in a karhai or heavy-based frying pan over medium heat and carefully fry the paneer until golden on all sides. Remove from the pan.

2 **Fry the onion** lightly in the same ghee, until softened and lightly golden. Remove the onion from the pan. Add 5 tablespoons hot water and a pinch of salt to the ghee and simmer for 1 minute. Add the peas and sugar, cover and cook for 5–6 minutes, until the peas are nearly cooked.

3 **Add the fried onion,** paneer, ginger, chilli and spring onion to the pan and cook for 2–3 minutes. Add the garam masala and coriander leaves. Season with salt, to taste.

SAAG PANEER

SERVES 4

500 g (1 lb 2 oz) English spinach leaves

½ teaspoon ground cumin

½ teaspoon ground coriander

½ teaspoon fenugreek seeds

1 tablespoon oil

1 red onion, thinly sliced

5 garlic cloves, chopped

200 g (7 oz) tinned chopped tomatoes

2 cm (¾ inch) piece of ginger, grated

1 teaspoon garam masala

225 g (8 oz) paneer, cubed

1   Blanch the spinach leaves in boiling water for 2 minutes, then refresh in cold water, drain and very finely chop. Place a small frying pan over low heat and dry-roast the cumin until aromatic. Remove, dry-roast the coriander, then the fenugreek.

2   Heat the oil in a karhai or heavy-based frying pan over low heat and fry the onion, garlic, cumin, coriander and fenugreek until brown and aromatic. Stir in the tomato, ginger and garam masala and bring to the boil. Add the spinach and cook until the liquid has reduced. Fold in the paneer, trying to keep it in whole pieces. Stir gently until heated through. Season with salt, to taste.

SMOKY SPICED EGGPLANT

SERVES 4

600 g (1 lb 5 oz) eggplants (aubergines)

1 red onion, chopped

1 garlic clove, chopped

2.5 cm (1 inch) piece of ginger, chopped

1 green chilli, chopped

80 ml (2½ fl oz) oil

¼ teaspoon chilli powder

½ teaspoon garam masala

2 teaspoons ground cumin

2 teaspoons ground coriander

2 teaspoons salt

½ teaspoon ground black pepper

2 ripe tomatoes, chopped

3–4 tablespoons coriander (cilantro) leaves, finely chopped

1 Scorch the eggplants by holding them over a medium gas flame, or heating them under a grill (broiler) or on an electric hotplate. Keep turning them until the skin is blackened on all sides. Set aside until cool, then peel off the charred skin. Roughly chop the flesh. Don't worry if black specks remain on the flesh because they add to the smoky flavour.

2 Combine the onion, garlic, ginger and chilli in a blender and process until chopped together but not a paste. Alternatively, chop finely with a knife and mix in a bowl.

3 Heat the oil in a deep, heavy-based frying pan over medium heat, add the onion mixture and cook until slightly browned. Add all the spices, and the salt and pepper, and stir for 1 minute. Add the chopped tomato and simmer until the liquid has reduced. Put the eggplants in the pan and mash them with a wooden spoon, stirring around with the spices. Simmer for 10 minutes, or until the eggplants are soft.

4 Stir in the chopped coriander leaves and season with salt, to taste.

GAJAR MATAR

SERVES 6

1 small onion, roughly chopped

1 garlic clove, roughly chopped

2.5 cm (1 inch) piece of ginger, chopped

125 ml (4 fl oz/½ cup) oil

1 teaspoon cumin seeds

1½ teaspoons ground turmeric

325 g (11½ oz) carrots, diced

1 teaspoon ground cumin

1 teaspoon ground coriander

250 g (9 oz/1⅔ cups) peas

3 teaspoons salt

¼ teaspoon sugar

¼ teaspoon chilli powder

4 teaspoons pomegranate seeds
  (optional)

½ teaspoon garam masala

1 **Put the onion,** garlic and ginger in a food processor and blend until finely chopped, or chop them with a knife and mix together.

2 **Heat the oil** in a karhai or frying pan, then add the onion mixture and stir over high heat for 2 minutes, or until softened. Reduce the heat to medium and add the cumin seeds and turmeric.

3 **When the seeds** are sizzling, add the carrot and stir for about 2 minutes. Add the ground cumin and coriander and fry for 2 minutes. Stir in the peas and then the salt, sugar and chilli powder. Add 2 tablespoons of water if using frozen peas, or 4 tablespoons if using fresh peas. Reduce the heat to a simmer, add the pomegranate seeds, if using, and stir before partially covering the pan. Simmer for 15 minutes, or until the carrot and peas are tender. Stir in the garam masala.

SAAG BHAJI

SERVES 4

200 g (7 oz) small turnips, finely chopped
1 kg (2 lb 4 oz) mixed English spinach and amaranth leaves, finely shredded
½ teaspoon chilli powder
1 tablespoon ghee or oil
2 cm (¾ inch) piece of ginger, grated
1 onion, finely chopped
1½ tablespoons lemon juice

1 **Bring** 125 ml (4 fl oz/½ cup) water to the boil in a large heavy-based saucepan over medium heat. Add the turnip, cook for 1–2 minutes, then add the spinach and amaranth. Stir in the chilli powder and a pinch of salt and cook for 2–3 minutes, or until almost all the water has evaporated. Mash the mixture well and remove from the heat.

2 **Heat the ghee** or oil in a heavy-based saucepan over low heat and fry the ginger and onion for 2–3 minutes. Add the mashed vegetables, mix well and keep tossing until everything is well mixed. Season with salt, to taste. Serve warm with a dash of lemon juice.

METHI ALOO

SERVES 4

1 small onion, roughly chopped

2 garlic cloves, roughly chopped

2.5 cm (1 inch) piece of ginger, roughly chopped

4 tablespoons oil

¼ teaspoon ground turmeric

600 g (1 lb 5 oz) potatoes, cut into cubes

2 green chillies, seeded and

finely chopped

¼ teaspoon chilli powder

½ teaspoon ground cumin

½ teaspoon ground coriander

3 teaspoons salt

½ teaspoon ground black pepper

140 g (5 oz) methi leaves, roughly chopped

unsalted butter (optional)

1 **Combine the onion,** garlic and ginger in a food processor and chop together, but not to a paste, or chop with a knife and mix together.

2 **Heat the oil** in a karhai or heavy-based frying pan over medium heat and fry the onion mixture until softened. Stir in the turmeric. Add the potato and chilli and fry for 5 minutes. Add the chilli powder, cumin, coriander, salt and pepper and stir for another minute.

3 **Add 2 tablespoons** water to the pan, cover, reduce the heat and simmer. As the potato cooks, it might start sticking to the pan, so after 10 minutes, add 2 more tablespoons of water if necessary. At no stage during the cooking time should the potato be allowed to brown.

4 **After another** 10 minutes, stir in the methi and cook over low heat for 15 minutes, or until the potato is soft (the type of potato you use will determine the length of cooking time). Season with salt, to taste. Serve with a knob of unsalted butter melted on top if you like.

STUFFED OKRA

SERVES 6

1 red onion, roughly chopped

4 garlic cloves, roughly chopped

10 cm (4 inch) piece of ginger, grated

5 teaspoons ground cumin

1 tablespoon ground coriander

2 teaspoons ground turmeric

1 teaspoon chilli powder

2 teaspoons garam masala

1 teaspoon ground black pepper

1 tablespoon salt

550 g (1 lb 4 oz) okra

125 ml (4 fl oz/½ cup) oil

pinch of asafoetida

1 Combine the onion, garlic and ginger in a food processor and blend them to form a paste, or chop them all finely and pound them together in a pestle and mortar. Transfer to a bowl and add 4 teaspoons of the cumin, the coriander, 1¼ teaspoons of the turmeric, the chilli powder and garam masala and mix well. Stir in the pepper and 3 teaspoons of the salt.

2 Cut off the bottoms of the okra, then use a knife to make a slit lengthwise in each of them, stopping just short of the tail end. Using your hands or a small knife, put a little of the spice mixture into the insides of the okra. Some of it will ooze out but don't worry. This process will take a little time but the end result is delicious. Carefully cut all the okra into 1 cm (½ inch) pieces, or if you prefer, you can leave them whole.

3 Heat the oil in a karhai or large, wide, heavy-based frying pan over low heat. Add the asafoetida and remaining turmeric to the pan and stir it around so that the oil absorbs the flavour. Add the okra and stir so it is coated in the flavoured oil. Add 2 tablespoons water.

4 Cover and cook for 10 minutes, shaking the pan occasionally to prevent the okra sticking to the pan (add 2 more tablespoons of water if necessary).

5 Add the remaining salt and remaining ground cumin to the pan. Shake the pan, then simmer the mixture for 5–10 minutes, until the okra is quite soft. The okra will retain a slight crunch on the outside because of its unique texture.

CAULIFLOWER WITH MUSTARD

SERVES 4

2 teaspoons yellow mustard seeds

2 teaspoons black mustard seeds

1 teaspoon ground turmeric

1 teaspoon tamarind purée

2–3 tablespoons mustard oil or oil

2 garlic cloves, finely chopped

½ onion, finely chopped

600 g (1 lb 5 oz) cauliflower, broken into small florets

3 mild green chillies, seeded and finely chopped

2 teaspoons kalonji (nigella seeds)

1 **Grind the mustard seeds** together to a fine powder in a spice grinder or pestle and mortar. Mix with the turmeric, tamarind purée and 125 ml (4 fl oz/½ cup) water to form a smooth, quite liquid paste.

2 **Heat 2 tablespoons** oil in a karhai or large, heavy-based saucepan over medium heat until almost smoking. Reduce the heat to low, add the garlic and onion and fry until golden. Cook the cauliflower in batches, adding more oil if necessary, and fry until lightly browned. Add the chilli and fry for 1 minute, or until tinged with brown around the edges.

3 **Return all the cauliflower** to the pan, sprinkle it with the mustard mixture and kalonji and stir well. Increase the heat to medium and bring to the boil, even though there's not much sauce. Reduce the heat to low, cover and cook until the cauliflower is nearly tender and the seasoning is dry. You may have to sprinkle a little more water on the cauliflower as it cooks to stop it sticking to the pan. If there is still excess liquid when the cauliflower is cooked, simmer with the lid off until it dries out. Season with salt, to taste, and remove from the heat.

AVIAL

SERVES 4

½ teaspoon ground turmeric

200 g (7 oz) carrots, cut into batons

200 g (7 oz) sweet potato, cut into batons

200 g (7 oz) green beans, topped and tailed and cut in half

50 g (1¾ oz) grated coconut

5 cm (2 inch) piece of ginger, grated

3 green chillies, finely chopped

1½ teaspoons ground cumin

420 ml (14½ fl oz/1⅔ cups) thick plain yoghurt

1 tablespoon oil

10 curry leaves

1 Bring 500 ml (17 fl oz/2 cups) water to the boil in a saucepan, add the turmeric and carrot, reduce the heat and simmer for 5 minutes. Add the sweet potato and the beans, return to the boil, then reduce the heat and simmer for 5 minutes, or until the vegetables are almost cooked.

2 Put the coconut, ginger and chilli in a blender or pestle and mortar, with a little water, and blend or grind to a paste. Add to the vegetables with the cumin and some salt and simmer for 2 minutes. Stir in the yoghurt and heat through.

3 For the final seasoning (tarka), heat the oil over low heat in a small saucepan. Add the curry leaves and allow to crisp. Pour the hot oil and the leaves over the vegetables.

CAULIFLOWER BHAJI

SERVES 4

1 teaspoon cumin seeds

3–4 tablespoons oil

¼ teaspoon black mustard seeds

250 g (9 oz) potatoes, cut into small cubes

750 g (1 lb 10 oz) cauliflower, broken into florets

½ teaspoon ground cumin

½ teaspoon ground coriander

¼ teaspoon ground turmeric

½ teaspoon garam masala

2 garlic cloves, finely chopped

2 green chillies, seeded and finely chopped

5 curry leaves

1 **Place a small frying pan** over low heat and dry-roast ¼ teaspoon of the cumin seeds until aromatic. Grind the roasted seeds to a fine powder using a pestle and mortar.

2 **Heat the oil** over low heat in a karhai or heavy-based saucepan. Add the mustard seeds and remaining cumin seeds, cover and allow to pop for a couple of seconds. Uncover, add the diced potato and fry for 1 minute, stirring occasionally to prevent the potato from sticking to the pan. Add the cauliflower, all the remaining spices, garlic, chilli and curry leaves and stir until well mixed. Add 60 ml (2 fl oz/ ¼ cup) water and bring to the boil. Cover and simmer for 5–7 minutes, or until the cauliflower is cooked and tender. Season with salt, to taste.

SPINACH KOFTA IN YOGHURT SAUCE

SERVES 6

YOGHURT SAUCE

375 ml (13 fl oz/1½ cups) thick plain yoghurt

4 tablespoons besan (chickpea flour)

1 tablespoon oil

2 teaspoons black mustard seeds

1 teaspoon fenugreek seeds

6 curry leaves

1 large onion, finely chopped

3 garlic cloves, crushed

1 teaspoon ground turmeric

½ teaspoon chilli powder

SPINACH KOFTAS

450 g (1 lb) English spinach, leaves picked off the stems, or 500 g (1 lb 2 oz) frozen spinach, thawed and drained

170 g (1½ cups) besan (chickpea flour)

1 red onion, finely chopped

1 ripe tomato, finely diced

2 garlic cloves, crushed

1 teaspoon ground cumin

2 tablespoons coriander (cilantro) leaves

oil, for deep-frying

coriander (cilantro) leaves (optional)

1 To make the yoghurt sauce, in a large bowl, whisk the yoghurt, besan flour and 750 ml (26 fl oz/3 cups) water to a smooth paste. Heat the oil in a heavy-based saucepan or deep frying pan over low heat. Add the mustard and fenugreek seeds and the curry leaves, cover and allow the seeds to pop for 1 minute. Add the onion and cook for 5 minutes, or until soft and starting to brown.

2 Add the garlic and stir for 1 minute, or until soft. Add the turmeric and chilli powder and stir for 30 seconds. Add the yoghurt mixture, bring to the boil and simmer over low heat for 10 minutes. Season with salt, to taste.

3 To make the spinach koftas, blanch the spinach in boiling water for 1 minute and refresh in cold water. Drain, squeeze out any extra water by putting the spinach between two plates and pushing them together. Finely chop the spinach. Combine with the remaining kofta ingredients and up to 60 ml (2 fl oz/¼ cup) of water, a little at a time, adding enough to make the mixture soft but not sloppy. If it becomes too sloppy, add more besan flour. Season with salt, to taste. (To test the seasoning, fry a small amount of the mixture and taste it.) Shape the mixture into balls by rolling it in dampened hands, using 1 tablespoon of mixture for each.

4 Fill a karhai or heavy-based saucepan one-third full with oil and heat to 180°C/350°F (a cube of bread will brown in 15 seconds). Lower the koftas into the oil in batches and fry until golden and crisp. Don't overcrowd the pan. Remove the koftas as they cook, shake off any excess oil and add them to the yoghurt sauce.

5 Gently reheat the yoghurt sauce and sprinkle with the coriander leaves if using.

CHANA MASALA

SERVES 6

250 g (9 oz) chickpeas

1 large onion, roughly chopped

2 garlic cloves, roughly chopped

5 cm (2 inch) piece of ginger, roughly chopped

1 green chilli, chopped

170 ml (5½ fl oz/⅔ cup) oil

1 tablespoon ground cumin

1 tablespoon ground coriander

1 teaspoon chilli powder

pinch of asafoetida

2 tablespoons thick plain yoghurt

2¼ tablespoons garam masala

2 teaspoons tamarind purée

½ lemon

3 green chillies, extra

¼ teaspoon ground black pepper

3 teaspoons salt

2 teaspoons chaat masala

½ red onion, sliced into thin rings

2 cm (¾ inch) piece of ginger, cut into thin strips

coriander (cilantro) leaves, roughly chopped (optional)

1 **Soak the chickpeas** overnight in 2 litres (70 fl oz/8 cups) of water. Drain, then put the chickpeas in a large saucepan with another 2 litres (70 fl oz/8 cups) water. Bring to the boil, spooning off any scum from the surface, then simmer over low heat for 1–1½ hours, until soft. It is important the chickpeas are soft at this stage as they won't soften once the sauce has been added. Drain, reserving the cooking liquid.

2 **Blend the onion,** garlic, ginger and chopped chilli to a paste in a food processor or very finely chop them together with a knife.

3 **Heat the oil in a heavy-based saucepan** over medium heat and fry the onion mixture until golden brown. Add the cumin, coriander, chilli powder and asafoetida, then stir for 1 minute. Add the yoghurt and stir for another minute.

4 **Stir in** 2 tablespoons of the garam masala and pour in 1.25 litres (44 fl oz/5 cups) of the reserved cooking liquid, a little at a time, stirring after each addition. Bring to the boil, then reduce the heat to simmering point.

5 **Add the tamarind purée,** lemon, whole chillies, chickpeas, pepper and the salt. Partially cover the pan, simmer for 30 minutes, then remove the lemon. Cook for another 30 minutes, or until all the liquid has reduced, leaving the softened chickpeas coated in a rich dark brown sauce.

6 **Add the chaat masala** and remaining garam masala and stir in the raw onion rings, ginger and coriander leaves if using.

TOOR DAL

SERVES 8

500 g (1 lb 2 oz) toor dal (yellow lentils)

5 x 5 cm (2 inch) pieces of kokum

2 teaspoons coriander seeds

2 teaspoons cumin seeds

2 tablespoons oil

2 teaspoons black mustard seeds

10 curry leaves

7 cloves

10 cm (4 inch) cinnamon stick

5 green chillies, finely chopped

½ teaspoon ground turmeric

400 g (14 oz) tinned chopped tomatoes

20 g (½ oz) jaggery or 10 g (¼ oz) molasses

coriander (cilantro) leaves

1 **Soak the lentils** in cold water for 2 hours. Rinse the kokum, remove any stones and put the kokum in a bowl with cold water for a few minutes to soften. Drain the lentils and put them in a heavy-based saucepan with 1 litre (35 fl oz/ 4 cups) of water and the pieces of kokum. Bring slowly to the boil, then simmer for about 40 minutes, or until the lentils feel soft when pressed between the thumb and index finger.

2 **Place a small frying pan** over low heat and dry-roast the coriander seeds until aromatic. Remove and dry-roast the cumin seeds. Grind the roasted seeds to a fine powder using a spice grinder or pestle and mortar.

3 **For the final seasoning** (tarka), heat the oil in a small pan over low heat. Add the mustard seeds and allow to pop. Add the curry leaves, cloves, cinnamon, chilli, turmeric and the roasted spice mix and cook for 1 minute. Add the tomato and cook for 2–3 minutes until the tomato is soft and can be broken up easily and incorporated into the sauce. Add the jaggery, then pour the spicy mixture into the simmering lentils and cook for another 10 minutes. Season with salt, to taste. Garnish with coriander leaves.

BLACK-EYED BEANS WITH MUSHROOMS

SERVES 6

200 g (7 oz) black-eyed beans

400 g (14 oz) ripe tomatoes or 400 g (14 oz) tinned chopped tomatoes

125 ml (4 fl oz/½ cup) oil

1 teaspoon cumin seeds

3 cm (1¼ inch) cinnamon stick

150 g (5½ oz) onion, chopped

4 garlic cloves, finely chopped

250 g (9 oz) mushrooms, sliced

2 teaspoons ground coriander

1 teaspoon ground cumin

½ teaspoon ground turmeric

¼ teaspoon cayenne pepper

2 tablespoons chopped coriander (cilantro) leaves

1 **Put the black-eyed beans** in a large saucepan with 1 litre (35 fl oz/4 cups) of water and bring to the boil. Cover and simmer for 2 minutes. Remove from the heat and leave to stand for 1 hour. Alternatively, if you prefer, you can soak the black-eyed beans overnight in the cold water.

2 **Score a cross** in the top of each ripe tomato. Plunge into boiling water for 20 seconds, then drain and peel away from the cross. Roughly chop the tomatoes, discarding the cores and seeds and reserving any juices.

3 **Bring the black-eyed beans** back to the boil, then simmer for 20–30 minutes, until tender. Drain well.

4 **Meanwhile,** heat the oil in a karhai or deep, heavy-based frying pan or saucepan. Add the cumin seeds and cinnamon stick, let them sizzle for 10 seconds, then add the onion and garlic. Stir over medium heat until soft and starting to brown. Add the mushrooms and fry for 2–3 minutes. Add the tomato, ground coriander, cumin, turmeric and cayenne pepper. Cover and cook over low heat for 10 minutes.

5 **Combine the black-eyed beans** with the tomato and mushroom mixture and season with salt, to taste. Stir in the coriander leaves and simmer, uncovered, for 30 minutes.

SWEET AND SOUR CHICKPEAS

SERVES 6

500 g (1 lb 2 oz/2¼ cups) chickpeas

2 tablespoons oil or ghee

2 large red onions, thinly sliced

2 cm (¾ inch) piece of ginger, finely chopped

2 teaspoons sugar

2 teaspoons ground coriander

2 teaspoons ground cumin

pinch of chilli powder (optional)

1 teaspoon garam masala

3 tablespoons tamarind purée

4 ripe tomatoes, chopped

4 tablespoons coriander (cilantro) or mint leaves, finely chopped

1 Soak the chickpeas overnight in 2 litres (70 fl oz/8 cups) water. Drain, then put the chickpeas in a large saucepan with 2 litres (70 fl oz/8 cups) water. Bring to the boil, spooning off any scum from the surface. Cover and simmer over low heat for 1–1½ hours, until soft. It is important they are soft at this stage as they won't soften once the sauce is added. Drain.

2 Heat the oil in a karhai or heavy-based frying pan. Fry the onion until soft and brown, then stir in the ginger. Add the chickpeas, sugar, coriander, cumin, chilli powder, garam masala and a pinch of salt. Stir, then add the tamarind and tomato and simmer for 2–3 minutes. Add 500 ml (17 fl oz/ 2 cups) water, bring to the boil and cook until the sauce has thickened. Stir in the coriander leaves. Serve with rotis.

CHOLE CHAAT

SERVES 4

220 g (7¾ oz/1 cup) chickpeas

2 tablespoons oil

½ onion, chopped

1 teaspoon ground coriander

1 teaspoon ground cumin

¼ teaspoon ground turmeric

1 teaspoon garam masala

2 cm (¾ inch) piece of ginger, grated

2 red chillies, finely chopped

200 g (7 oz) tinned chopped tomatoes, drained

1 **Soak the chickpeas overnight** in 2 litres (70 fl oz/8 cups) water. Drain, then put the chickpeas in a large saucepan with 2 litres (8 cups) water. Bring to the boil, spooning off any scum from the surface, then simmer over low heat for 1–1½ hours, until soft. It is important the chickpeas are soft at this stage as they won't soften any more once the sauce has been added. Drain, reserving the cooking liquid. Remove 6 tablespoons of the chickpeas and thoroughly mash them with a fork.

2 **Heat the oil** in a heavy-based saucepan over low heat and cook the onion until golden brown. Add the coriander, cumin, turmeric and garam masala and fry for 1 minute. Add ginger, chilli, tomato and salt, to taste, and stir until well mixed. Add the chickpeas and their cooking liquid, and the mashed chickpeas. Bring to the boil, reduce the heat and simmer, uncovered, for 5 minutes.

URAD DAL

SERVES 4

250 g (9 oz) unskinned urad dal

¼ teaspoon ground turmeric

4 ripe tomatoes, chopped

1 small onion, roughly chopped

2 tablespoons oil

½ teaspoon cumin seeds

1 teaspoon fennel seeds

5 cm (2 inch) piece of ginger, grated

2 dried chillies, broken into pieces

pinch of asafoetida

coriander (cilantro) leaves, to garnish

1 **Put the dal in a heavy-based saucepan** and add 1 litre (35 fl oz/4 cups) water, the turmeric, chopped tomato and onion. Bring to the boil, then reduce the heat, cover and simmer for about 40 minutes, or until the dal is cooked and feels soft when pressed between the thumb and index finger.

2 **For the final seasoning** (tarka), heat the oil in a small saucepan, add the cumin and fennel seeds and allow to pop. Add the ginger, chilli and asafoetida and fry over low heat for 30 seconds. Pour into the hot dal and simmer for another 5 minutes. Season with salt, to taste. Garnish with coriander leaves before serving.

DAL SAAG

SERVES 4

225 g (8 oz) moong dal

2–3 tablespoons oil

1 teaspoon black mustard seeds

8 curry leaves

¼ teaspoon asafoetida

¼ teaspoon ground turmeric

1 teaspoon ground cumin

1 teaspoon ground coriander

3 cm (1¼ inch) piece of ginger, grated

2 green chillies, seeded and cut into 1 cm (½ inch) pieces

100 g (3½ oz) English spinach leaves, roughly chopped

5 spring onions (scallions), finely chopped

1 **Put the moong dal** in a heavy-based saucepan, add 750 ml (26 fl oz/3 cups) water and bring to the boil. Reduce the heat and simmer for 30 minutes, or until the moong dal are soft and breaking up. The moong dal tend to soak up most of the liquid so you may need to add a little more.

2 **For the final seasoning** (tarka), heat the oil in a saucepan, add the mustard seeds, cover and allow to pop. Stir in the curry leaves, asafoetida, turmeric, cumin, coriander, ginger and chilli, then pour into the cooked dal.

3 **Stir in the spinach** and spring onion and cook for about 2 minutes, or until the spinach is just cooked. Season with salt, to taste.

KALI DAL

SERVES 6

250 g (9 oz) whole black gram (sabat urad)

1 onion, roughly chopped

2 garlic cloves, roughly chopped

5 cm (2 inch) piece of ginger, roughly chopped

1 green chilli, roughly chopped

125 ml (4 fl oz/½ cup) oil

2 tablespoons ground cumin

1 tablespoon ground coriander

2 teaspoons salt

¼ teaspoon chilli powder

3 tablespoons garam masala

125 ml (4 fl oz/½ cup) cream

1 Put the whole black gram in a large, heavy-based saucepan, add 2 litres (70 fl oz/8 cups) water and bring to the boil. Reduce the heat and simmer for 1 hour, or until the dal feels soft when pressed between the thumb and index finger. Most of the dal will split to reveal the creamy insides. Drain, reserving the cooking liquid.

2 Blend the onion, garlic, ginger and chilli together in a food processor to form a paste, or finely chop them together with a knife. Heat the oil in a frying pan and fry the onion mixture over high heat, stirring constantly, until golden brown. Add the cumin and coriander and fry for 2 minutes. Add the dal and stir in the salt, chilli powder and garam masala. Pour 310 ml (10¾ fl oz/1¼ cups) of the reserved dal liquid into the pan, bring to the boil, then reduce the heat and simmer for 10 minutes. Just before serving, stir in the cream and simmer for another 2 minutes to heat through.

MASALA RAJMA

SERVES 4

225 g (8 oz) kidney beans

3 tablespoons oil

½ onion, finely chopped

2 Indian bay leaves (cassia leaves)

5 cm (2 inch) cinnamon stick

2 garlic cloves, finely chopped

¼ teaspoon ground turmeric

½ teaspoon ground coriander

½ teaspoon ground cumin

½ teaspoon garam masala

3 dried chillies

2 cm (¾ inch) piece of ginger, grated

1   **Soak the kidney beans** overnight in 1.25 litres (44 fl oz/ 5 cups) water in a large saucepan. Drain, return the beans to the saucepan with 1.25 litres (44 fl oz/5 cups) water and bring to the boil. Boil for 15 minutes, then reduce the heat and simmer for 1 hour, or until the beans are tender. Drain, reserving the liquid.

2   **Heat the oil** in a heavy-based saucepan over low heat. Add the onion, bay leaves, cinnamon and garlic and cook until the onion is lightly browned. Add the turmeric, coriander, cumin, garam masala, chillies and ginger and stir well. Add the beans with enough of their liquid to make a sauce.

3   **Bring to the boil** and cook for 5 minutes, stirring constantly. Season with salt, to taste. If you wish, remove the chillies before serving.

PARIPPU

SERVES 4

225 g (8 oz) masoor dal (red lentils)
1 onion, roughly chopped
1 ripe tomato, roughly chopped
50 g (1¾ oz) creamed coconut, mixed with 250 ml (9 fl oz/1 cup) water, or 250 ml (9 fl oz/1 cup) coconut milk
2 green chillies, chopped
¼ teaspoon ground turmeric
½ teaspoon ground cumin
½ teaspoon ground coriander
2 tablespoons oil
1 teaspoon cumin seeds
½ teaspoon black mustard seeds
1 onion, very finely chopped
10 curry leaves

1 Put the lentils in a heavy-based saucepan with 500 ml (17 fl oz/2 cups) water. Add the roughly chopped onion, tomato, creamed coconut or coconut milk, green chilli, turmeric, ground cumin and coriander, and bring to the boil. Simmer and cook, stirring occasionally, until the lentils are cooked to a soft mush (masoor dal does not hold its shape when it cooks). This will take about 25 minutes. If all the water has evaporated before the lentils are cooked, add 125 ml (4 fl oz/½ cup) boiling water.

2 For the final seasoning (tarka), heat the oil in a small saucepan over low heat. Add the cumin seeds and mustard seeds, cover and allow the seeds to pop. Add the finely chopped onion and curry leaves and fry over low heat until the onion is golden brown. Pour the seasoned onions into the simmering lentils. Season with salt, to taste, and cook for another 5 minutes.

RICE & GRAINS

PULAO

SERVES 6

500 g (1 lb 2 oz/2½ cups) basmati rice

1 teaspoon cumin seeds

4 tablespoons ghee or oil

2 tablespoons chopped almonds

2 tablespoons raisins or sultanas

2 onions, finely sliced

2 cinnamon sticks

5 cardamom pods

1 teaspoon sugar

1 tablespoon ginger juice

15 saffron threads, soaked in

1 tablespoon warm milk

2 Indian bay leaves (cassia leaves)

250 ml (9 fl oz/1 cup) coconut milk

2 tablespoons fresh or frozen peas

rosewater (optional)

1 **Wash the rice in a sieve under cold,** running water until the water from the rice runs clear. Drain the rice and put in a saucepan, cover with water and soak for 30 minutes. Drain.

2 **Place a small frying pan** over low heat and dry-roast the cumin seeds until aromatic.

3 **Heat the ghee** or oil in a karhai or heavy-based frying pan and fry the almonds and raisins until browned. Remove from the pan, fry the onion in the same ghee until dark golden brown, then remove from the pan.

4 **Add the rice,** roasted cumin seeds, cinnamon, cardamom, sugar, ginger juice, saffron and salt to the pan and fry for 2 minutes, or until aromatic.

5 **Add the bay leaves** and coconut milk to the pan, then add enough water to come about 5 cm (2 inches) above the rice. Bring to the boil, cover and cook over medium heat for 8 minutes, or until most of the water has evaporated.

6 **Add the peas** to the pan and stir well. Reduce the heat to very low and cook until the rice is cooked through. Stir in the fried almonds, raisins and onion, reserving some for garnishing. Drizzle with a few drops of rosewater if you would like a more perfumed dish.

UPAMA

SERVES 4

2 tablespoons chana dal

4 tablespoons ghee or oil

75 g (2½ oz/½ cup) cashew nuts

1 teaspoon black mustard seeds

15 curry leaves

½ onion, finely chopped

140 g (5 oz/1½ cups) coarse semolina

lime juice, to serve

1 Soak the dal in plenty of water for 3 hours. Drain, then put in a saucepan with 500 ml (17 fl oz/2 cups) water. Bring to the boil and cook for 2 minutes. Drain the dal, then dry in a tea towel. Brush a little of the ghee onto the cashew nuts and toast them in a frying pan over low heat until they are golden.

2 Heat the remaining ghee in a heavy-based frying pan and add the mustard seeds and dal. Cook until the seeds start to pop, add the curry leaves and onion and cook until the onion softens. Add the semolina. Toss everything together and when the semolina is hot and the grains are brown and coated in oil, sprinkle with 500 ml (17 fl oz/2 cups) boiling water, 125 ml (4 fl oz/½ cup) at a time, tossing and stirring after each addition, until absorbed. Season with salt. Sprinkle with lime juice and cashews.

KHICHHARI

SERVES 6

60 g (2¼ oz/¼ cup) toor dal (yellow lentils)

300 g (10½ oz/1½ cups) basmati rice

3 tablespoons ghee

1 teaspoon cumin seeds

6 cloves

½ cinnamon stick

2 onions, finely chopped

2 garlic cloves, finely chopped

2 cm (¾ inch) piece of ginger, finely chopped

1 teaspoon garam masala

3 tablespoons lemon juice

1 teaspoon salt

1 **Soak the dal** in 500 ml (17 fl oz/2 cups) water in a large saucepan for 2 hours. Wash the rice in a sieve under cold water until the water from the rice runs clear. Drain.

2 **Heat the ghee** in a heavy-based saucepan over low heat and fry the cumin seeds, cloves and cinnamon for a few seconds. Increase the heat to medium, add the onion, garlic and ginger and cook until they soften and begin to brown.

3 **Add the rice** and dal and toss to thoroughly coat in ghee. Add the garam masala, lemon juice, salt and 750 ml (26 fl oz/ 3 cups) boiling water. Bring to the boil, then reduce the heat to very low, cover tightly and cook for 15 minutes. Remove from the heat and gently fluff up with a fork. Cover the pan with a clean cloth and leave for 10 minutes. Fluff up again and season with salt, to taste.

LAMB BIRYANI

SERVES 6

1 kg (2 lb 4 oz) boneless lamb
   leg or shoulder, cut into 3 cm
   (1¼ inch) cubes

8 cm (3 inch) piece of ginger, grated

2 garlic cloves, crushed

2 tablespoons garam masala

½ teaspoon chilli powder

½ teaspoon ground turmeric

4 green chillies, finely chopped

20 g (¾ oz) chopped coriander (cilantro)
   leaves

15 g (½ oz) chopped mint leaves

500 g (1 lb 2 oz/2½ cups) basmati rice

4 onions, thinly sliced

¼ teaspoon salt

125 ml (4 fl oz/½ cup) oil

125 g (4½ oz) unsalted butter, melted

250 ml (9 fl oz/1 cup) thick plain yoghurt

½ teaspoon saffron strands, soaked in
   2 tablespoons hot milk

3 tablespoons lemon juice

SEALING DOUGH

200 g (7 oz/1⅓ cups) wholewheat flour

1 teaspoon salt

1 Mix the lamb cubes in a bowl with the ginger, garlic, garam masala, chilli powder, turmeric, chilli, coriander and mint. Cover and marinate in the fridge overnight.

2 Wash the rice in a sieve under cold, running water until the water from the rice runs clear. Put the sliced onion in a sieve, sprinkle with the salt and leave for 10 minutes to drain off any liquid that oozes out. Rinse and pat dry.

3 Heat the oil and butter in a large, heavy-based saucepan, add the onion and fry for about 10 minutes or until golden brown. Drain through a sieve, reserving the oil and butter.

4 Remove the lamb from the marinade, reserving the marinade, and fry in batches in a little of the oil and butter until the lamb is browned. Transfer to a heavy casserole and add the onion, any remaining marinade and the yoghurt, and cook over low heat for 30–40 minutes, or until the lamb is tender.

5 In a separate saucepan, boil enough water to cover the rice. Add the rice to the pan. Return the water to the boil, cook the rice for 5 minutes, then drain well and spread the rice evenly over the meat. Pour 2 tablespoons of the leftover oil and ghee over the rice and drizzle with the saffron and milk.

6 To make the sealing dough, preheat the oven to 220°C (425°F/Gas 7). Make a dough by mixing the flour and salt with a little water. Roll the dough into a sausage shape and use to seal the lid onto the rim of the pot or casserole, pressing it along the rim where the lid meets the pot. Put the pot over high heat for 5 minutes to bring the contents to the boil, then transfer it to the oven for 40 minutes. Remove the pot and break the seal of dough.

YAKHNI PULAO

SERVES 4

225 g (8 oz) basmati rice

500 ml (17 fl oz/2 cups) chicken stock

6 tablespoons ghee or oil

5 cardamom pods

5 cm (2 inch) cinnamon stick

6 cloves

8 black peppercorns

4 Indian bay leaves (cassia leaves)

1 onion, finely sliced

1 Wash the rice in a sieve under cold running water until the water from the rice runs clear. Drain. heat the stock to near boiling point in a saucepan.

2 Meanwhile, heat 2 tablespoons of the ghee or oil over medium heat in a large, heavy-based saucepan. Add the cardamom, cinnamon, cloves, peppercorns and bay leaves and fry for 1 minute. Reduce the heat to low, add the rice and stir constantly for 1 minute. Add the heated stock and some salt to the rice and bring rapidly to the boil. Cover and simmer over low heat for 15 minutes. Leave the rice to stand for 10 minutes before uncovering. Lightly fluff up the rice before serving.

3 Meanwhile, heat the remaining ghee or oil in a frying pan over low heat and fry the onion until soft. Increase the heat and fry until the onion is dark brown. Drain on paper towels, then use as garnish.

PRAWN PULAO

SERVES 4

200 g (7 oz/1 cup) basmati rice

300 g (10½ oz) small prawns (shrimp)

3 tablespoons oil

1 onion, finely chopped

3 cm (1¼ inch) cinnamon stick

6 cardamom pods

5 cloves

4 Indian bay leaves (cassia leaves)

1 stalk lemongrass, finely chopped

4 garlic cloves, crushed

5 cm (2 inch) piece of ginger, grated

¼ teaspoon ground turmeric

1 **Wash the rice** in a sieve under cold running water until the water from the rice runs clear. Drain. Peel and devein the prawns, then wash thoroughly and pat dry with paper towels.

2 **Heat the oil** in a karhai or heavy-based frying pan over low heat and fry the onion, cinnamon, cardamom, cloves, bay leaves and lemongrass until the onion is lightly browned. Stir in the garlic, ginger and turmeric. Add the prawns and stir until they turn pinkish. Add the rice and fry over medium heat for 2 minutes. Add 500 ml (17 fl oz/2 cups) boiling water and some salt and bring to the boil. Reduce the heat and simmer for 15 minutes. Remove from the heat, cover tightly with a lid and leave for 10 minutes. Fluff up the rice before serving.

YOGHURT RICE

SERVES 4

2 tablespoons urad dal

2 tablespoons chana dal

225 g (8 oz) basmati rice

2 tablespoons oil

½ teaspoon mustard seeds

12 curry leaves

3 dried chillies

¼ teaspoon ground turmeric

pinch of asafoetida

500 ml (17 fl oz/2 cups) thick plain
   yoghurt

1   **Soak the dals** in 250 ml (9 fl oz/1 cup) boiling water for
3 hours. Wash the rice in a sieve under cold running water
until the water from the rice runs clear. Drain.

2   **Put the rice** and 500 ml (17 fl oz/2 cups) water in a
saucepan and bring rapidly to the boil. Stir, cover, reduce the
heat to a slow simmer and cook for 10 minutes. Leave for
15 minutes before fluffing up with a fork.

3   **Drain the dals** and pat dry with paper towels. For the final
seasoning (tarka), heat the oil in a small saucepan over low
heat, add the mustard seeds, cover and shake the pan until the
seeds start to pop. Add the curry leaves, chillies and the dals
and fry for 2 minutes, stirring occasionally. Stir in the turmeric
and asafoetida.

4   **Put the yoghurt** in a large bowl, pour the fried dal mixture
into the yoghurt and mix thoroughly. Mix the rice into the
spicy yoghurt. Season with salt, to taste. Cover and refrigerate.
Serve cold, but before serving, stand the rice at room
temperature for about 10 minutes. Serve as part of a meal.
Yoghurt rice goes very well with meat dishes.

ANDHRA-STYLE CHICKEN PULAO

SERVES 8

1.5 kg (3 lb 5 oz) chicken or chicken pieces

1 kg (2 lb 4 oz/5 cups) basmati rice

3 onions, sliced

½ teaspoon salt

125 ml (4 fl oz/½ cup) oil

180 g (6 oz) ghee

4 cm (1½ inch) cinnamon stick

2 cardamom pods

3 cloves

2 star anise

2 stalks of curry leaves

2 cm (¾ inch) piece of ginger, grated

6 garlic cloves, crushed

4–6 green chillies, slit lengthwise

420 ml (14½ fl oz/1⅔ cups) buttermilk

4 ripe tomatoes, diced

185 ml (6 fl oz/¾ cup) coconut milk

1 litre (35 fl oz/4 cups) chicken stock

1 lemon, cut into wedges

1   **If using a whole chicken,** cut it into 16 pieces by removing both legs and cutting between the joint of the drumstick and thigh. Cut each of these in half through the bone.

2   **Cut down either side** of the backbone and remove the backbone. Turn the chicken over and cut through the cartilage down the centre of the breastbone. Cut each breast into 3 pieces and cut off the wings. Trim off the wing tips. and excess fat or skin.

3   **Wash the rice** in a sieve under cold, running water until the water from the rice runs clear. Drain well. Put the sliced onion in a sieve, sprinkle with the salt and leave for 10 minutes to drain off any liquid that oozes out. Rinse and pat dry.

4   **Heat the oil and ghee** over medium heat in a large, ovenproof 'degchi' (thick-based pot), or heavy casserole. Add the cinnamon, cardamom and cloves and heat until they begin to crackle. Reduce the heat to low and add the star anise and

the curry leaves from one stem. Add the sliced onion and cook until golden brown. Add the ginger and garlic and cook until golden. Add the chicken, increase the heat to medium and fry until the pieces are browned on all sides. Add the slit chillies, the remaining curry leaves, the buttermilk and some salt. Cook for 12 minutes, or until the chicken is cooked through and the liquid is reduced by half. Add the diced tomato and the coconut milk. Cook until the tomato is tender, then add the stock and bring to the boil.

5   **Preheat the oven** to 220°C (425°F/Gas 7). Add the drained rice to the chicken and stir well. Check the seasoning, adjust if necessary, and cook for 10 minutes, or until nearly all the liquid is absorbed. Remove the pot from the heat, cover it with a cloth, then a tight-fitting lid, and put it in the oven for 15 minutes, until the rice is cooked through.

SEVIAN KHEEMA

SERVES 4

1 teaspoon cumin seeds

3 tablespoons ghee or oil

1 red onion, finely chopped

3 garlic cloves, crushed

2 cm (¾ inch) piece of ginger, grated

225 g (8 oz) minced (ground) lamb or beef

1 teaspoon ground black pepper

225 g (8 oz) sevian noodles, broken into small pieces

3 tablespoons lime or lemon juice

1 Place a small frying pan over low heat, dry-roast the cumin until aromatic, then grind to a fine powder using a spice grinder or pestle and mortar.

2 Heat 1 tablespoon ghee in a karhai or heavy-based frying pan and fry the onion, garlic and ginger for 3–4 minutes. Add the cumin, cook for 1 minute, then add the meat and cook for 8 minutes, or until the meat is dry, breaking up any lumps with the back of a fork. Season with the black pepper and salt, to taste, and remove from the pan.

3 Heat the remaining ghee and fry the sevian for about 2 minutes. Add the meat and fry for 1 minute. Add 170 ml (5½ fl oz/⅔ cup) water and cook until the sevian are tender, adding more water if necessary. The dish should be dry, so don't add too much at once. When cooked, sprinkle with the juice.

IDIYAPPAM

SERVES 4

225 g (8 oz) rice sticks or vermicelli

4 tablespoons oil

50 g (2 oz) cashew nuts

½ onion, chopped

3 eggs

150 g (5½ oz/1 cup) fresh or frozen peas

10 curry leaves

2 carrots, grated

2 leeks, finely shredded

1 red capsicum (pepper), diced

2 tablespoons tomato sauce (ketchup)

1 tablespoon soy sauce

1 teaspoon salt

1   Soak the rice sticks in cold water for 30 minutes, then drain and put them in a saucepan of boiling water. Remove from the heat and leave in the pan for 3 minutes. Drain and refresh in cold water.

2   Heat 1 tablespoon oil in a frying pan and fry the cashews until golden. Remove, add the onion to the pan, fry until dark golden, then drain on paper towels. Cook the eggs in boiling water for 10 minutes to hard-boil, then cool them immediately in cold water. When cold, peel them and cut into wedges. Cook the peas in boiling water until tender.

3   Heat the remaining oil in a frying pan and briefly fry the curry leaves. Add the carrot, leek and red capsicum and stir for 1 minute. Add the tomato sauce, soy sauce, salt and rice sticks and mix, stirring constantly to prevent the rice sticks from sticking to the pan. Serve on a platter and garnish with the peas, cashews, fried onion and egg.

BREADS

CHAPATIS

MAKES 8

200 g (7 oz/1⅓ cups) atta (chapati flour)

½ teaspoon salt

100 g (3½ oz) ghee or clarified butter

1 Sift the atta and salt into a bowl and make a well in the centre. Add about 170 ml (5½ fl oz/⅔ cup) tepid water, enough to mix to form a soft, pliable dough. Turn the dough out onto a floured work surface and knead for 5 minutes. Place in an oiled bowl, cover and allow to rest for 30 minutes.

2 Put a tava or griddle, or a heavy-based frying pan over medium heat and leave it to heat up. Divide the dough into eight equal portions. Working with one portion at a time and keeping the rest covered, on a lightly floured surface roll out each portion to form a 15 cm (6 inch) diameter circle. Keep the rolled chapatis covered with a damp cloth while you roll them and cook them. Remove the excess surface flour on the chapati prior to cooking by holding the chapati in the palms of your hands and gently slapping it from one hand to the other. If you leave the flour on it may burn.

3 Place each chapati on the tava, leave it for 7–10 seconds to brown, then turn it over to brown on the other side. Depending on the hotness of the griddle, the second side should take about 15 seconds. Turn over the chapati again and, using a folded tea towel, apply gentle pressure to the chapati in several places to heat it and encourage it to puff up like a balloon. It is this puffing up process that gives the chapati its light texture. Smear the hot chapati with a little of the ghee or butter, and leave stacked and covered with a tea towel until all the chapatis are cooked.

NAAN

MAKES 10

500 g (1 lb 2 oz/4 cups) maida or plain (all-purpose) flour
310 ml (10¾ fl oz/1¼ cups) milk
2 teaspoons (7 g/¼ oz) easy-blend dried yeast or 15 g (½ oz) fresh yeast
2 teaspoons kalonji (nigella seeds), (optional)
½ teaspoon baking powder
½ teaspoon salt
1 egg, beaten
2 tablespoons oil or ghee
185 ml (6 fl oz/¾ cup) thick plain yoghurt

1 Sift the maida into a large bowl and make a well in the centre. Warm the milk over low heat in a saucepan until it is hand hot. If you are using fresh yeast, mix it with a little milk and a pinch of maida and set it aside to activate and go frothy.

2 Add the yeast, kalonji, baking powder and salt to the maida. In another bowl, mix the egg, oil and yoghurt. Pour into the maida with 250 ml (1 cup) of the milk and mix to form a soft dough. If the dough seems dry add the remaining milk. Turn out onto a floured work surface and knead for 5 minutes, or until smooth and elastic. Put in an oiled bowl, cover and leave in a warm place to double in size.

3 Preheat the oven to 200°C (400°F/Gas 6). Place a roasting tin half-filled with water at the bottom of the oven. This provides moisture in the oven which prevents the naan from drying out too quickly.

4 Punch down the dough, knead it briefly and divide it into 10 portions. Using the tips of your fingers, spread out one portion of dough to the shape of a naan bread. They are traditionally tear-drop in shape, so pull the dough on one end. Put the naan on a greased baking tray. Bake on the top shelf for 7 minutes, then turn the naan over and cook for another 5 minutes. While the first naan is cooking, shape the next one. If your tray is big enough, you may be able to fit two naan at a time. Remove the cooked naan from the oven and cover with a cloth to keep it warm and soft.

5 Repeat the cooking process until all the dough is used. You can only use the top shelf of the oven because the naan won't cook properly on the middle shelf. Refill the baking tray with boiling water when necessary.

PARATHAS

MAKES 6

200 g (7 oz/1⅓ cups) atta (chapati flour)

½ teaspoon salt

1 tablespoon oil or ghee

oil or ghee, for cooking and brushing

1 **Sift the atta** and the salt into a bowl and make a well in the centre. Add about 170 ml (5½ fl oz/⅔ cup) tepid water and the oil or ghee and mix to form a soft pliable dough. Turn the dough out onto a floured work surface and knead for 5 minutes, then place in an oiled bowl, cover and allow to rest for 30 minutes. Divide the dough into six equal portions.

2 **Roll each portion** into a 15 cm (6 inch) diameter circle. Using a pastry brush, cover the surface of each paratha with a very thin coating of oil or ghee. Fold each into a semicircle and brush thinly with oil. Fold into quarters and roll out each quarter to roughly three times its original size. Cover the rolled-out parathas with a cloth and cook them one at a time.

3 **Place a tava**, griddle or a heavy-based frying pan over medium heat and leave it to heat up. Lightly brush the surface of the tava or griddle with oil. Remove the excess surface flour on each paratha prior to cooking by holding it in the palms of your hands and gently slapping it from one hand to the other. If you leave the flour on, it may burn.

4 **Put a paratha** on the tava and cook for 1 minute. Turn it over and cook for another minute, or until the surface has brown flecks. This cooking process should be quick to ensure that the parathas remain soft. Repeat until all the parathas are cooked. Cover the cooked ones with a cloth.

5 **Parathas must be served warm** and can be reheated in a microwave oven, or wrapped in foil and heated in a conventional oven at 180°C (350°F/Gas 4) for 10 minutes.

PURIS

MAKES 12 LARGE OR 35 CRISPS

325 g (11½ oz/2⅔ cups) maida or plain (all-purpose) flour

125 g (4½ oz/1 cup) fine semolina

oil, for deep-frying

1 Mix the maida and semolina with 125 ml (½ cup) water into a dough and knead well until firm. If necessary, add more flour to make it a really firm dough. Cover and leave for 1 hour.

2 To make puri, knead the dough again, then divide into 12 balls. Roll each dough ball out to 1 mm thick (not too thin), making a circle about 10 cm in diameter.

3 Fill a karhai or heavy-based saucepan one-third full with oil and heat to 180°C/350°F. Test the temperature by putting a small piece of the dough into the oil. If the dough rises to the surface in a couple of seconds, the oil is ready. Put a puri into the hot oil, then about 5 seconds after it rises to the surface, gently push it down, using the back of a spoon, to keep it submerged in the hot oil until it puffs up—this will also take about 5 seconds. Turn over and cook until the other side is

lightly browned. Remove from the oil and drain on a wire rack. This whole frying process should take 15–20 seconds for each puri. Continue until all the puris are cooked.

4 To make puri crisps, roll out the kneaded dough to 1 mm (not too thin), cut out 4 cm diameter circles with a pastry cutter and set them aside on a tray.

5 Fill a karhai or heavy-based saucepan one-third full with oil and heat until a small ball of dough will rise to the surface in a few seconds. Deep-fry the puri crisps in batches until golden and puffed. Drain on paper towels. If you have any remaining pastry, cut it into pieces and deep-fry to make irregular-shaped crisps.

SAAG ROTI

MAKES 20

200 g (7 oz) English spinach leaves, stalks removed

500 g (1 lb 2 oz/3⅓ cups) atta (chapati flour)

1 teaspoon salt

1 teaspoon ghee or oil

ghee or oil for cooking

1 **Cook the spinach** briefly in a little simmering water until it is just wilted, then refresh in cold water. Drain thoroughly, then finely chop. Squeeze out any extra water by putting the spinach between two plates and pushing them together.

2 **Sift the atta** and salt into a bowl and make a well in the centre. Add the spinach, ghee and about 250 ml (9 fl oz/1 cup) tepid water and mix to form a soft, pliable dough. Turn out the dough onto a floured work surface and knead for 5 minutes. Place in an oiled bowl, cover and allow to rest for 30 minutes.

3 **Divide the dough** into 20 balls. Working with one portion at a time and keeping the rest covered, on a lightly floured surface evenly roll out each portion to a 12 cm (5 inch) circle about 1 mm (½₂ inch) thick.

4 **Heat a tava,** griddle or heavy-based frying pan until hot, oil it lightly with ghee or oil and cook one roti at a time. Cook each on one side, covered with a saucepan lid (this will help keep them soft), for about 1 minute. Turn it over, cover again and cook the other side for 2 minutes. Check the roti a few times to make sure it doesn't overcook. The roti will blister a little and brown in some places. Remove the roti and keep it warm under a tea towel. Cook the remaining roti

STUFFED PARATHAS

MAKES 14

400 g (2²/₃ cups) atta (chapati flour)
1 teaspoon salt
4 tablespoons oil or ghee
200 g (7 oz) potatoes, unpeeled
¼ teaspoon mustard seeds
½ onion, finely chopped
pinch of ground turmeric
pinch of asafoetida
ghee or oil for shallow-frying
extra ghee or oil for brushing on the dough

1 Sift the atta and salt into a bowl and make a well in the centre. Add 2 tablespoons of the oil or ghee and about 310 ml (10¾ fl oz/1¼ cups) tepid water and mix to a soft, pliable dough. Turn out onto a floured surface, knead for 5 minutes, then place in an oiled bowl. Cover and allow to rest for 30 minutes.

2 Simmer the potatoes for 15–20 minutes or until cooked. Cool slightly, then peel and mash. Heat the remaining oil or ghee in a saucepan over medium heat, add the mustard seeds, cover and shake the pan until the seeds start to pop. Add the onion and fry for 1 minute. Stir in the turmeric and asafoetida. Mix in the potato and cook over low heat for 1–2 minutes, or until the mixture leaves the side of the pan. Leave to cool.

3 Divide the dough into 14 portions and roll each into a 15 cm (6 inch) circle. Spread 1 teaspoon of the potato filling evenly over one half of each circle of dough and fold into a semicircle. Rub oil on half the surface area, then fold over into quarters. Roll out until doubled in size. Cover the parathas with a cloth, then cook them one at a time.

4 Heat a tava, griddle or a heavy-based frying pan over medium heat. Brush the surface of the tava or griddle with oil. Remove the excess flour on each paratha prior to cooking.

5 Cook each paratha for 2–3 minutes, then turn over and cook for 1 minute, or until the surface has brown flecks. Cooking should be quick to ensure the parathas stay soft. Cover the cooked parathas with a cloth. Serve warm. Reheat in a microwave, or wrap in foil and heat in a conventional oven at 180°C (350°F/Gas 4) for 10 minutes.

QUICK IDLIS

MAKES 16

50 g (1¾ oz) chana dal

2 cm (¾ inch) piece of ginger, finely chopped

310 g (11 oz/1¼ cups) thick plain yoghurt

2 tablespoons oil

1 teaspoon black mustard seeds

10 curry leaves

1 green chilli, seeded and finely chopped

300 g (10½ oz/2½ cups) fine semolina

25 g (1 oz) grated coconut

¼ teaspoon baking soda

2 teaspoons salt

1   Put the dal in a bowl, cover with water and soak for at least 4 hours, or overnight. Drain and blend with the ginger, yoghurt and 170 ml (5½ fl oz/⅔ cup) water in a food processor or blender, to form a loose paste.

2   Heat the oil in a frying pan, add the mustard seeds, cover and shake the pan until the seeds start to pop. Add the curry leaves and chilli and fry for 1 minute. Add the semolina and grated coconut and stir for about 2 minutes, or until they start to brown.

3   Mix both the mixtures together and stir in the baking soda and salt. Leave for about 1 hour, until the mixture thickens and becomes fluffy. Add enough water, about 625 ml (21½ fl oz/2½ cups), to make a thick, pourable batter. Pour the mixture into a greased idli mould, filling the cups almost full.

4   Cover and steam the idlis over simmering water for 10 minutes, or until they are firm and puffed.

DOSAS

MAKES 20

110 g (4 oz) urad dal

1 teaspoon salt

300 g (10 oz/1¾ cups) rice flour

oil for cooking

1 Put the dal in a bowl and cover with water. Soak for at least 4 hours or overnight.

2 Drain, then grind the dal with the salt and a little water in a food processor, blender or pestle and mortar to form a fine paste. Mix the paste with the rice flour, add 1 litre water and mix well. Cover with a cloth and leave in a warm place for 8 hours, or until the batter ferments and bubbles. The batter will double in volume.

3 Heat a tava or a non-stick frying pan over medium heat and leave to heat up. Don't overheat it—the heat should always be medium. Lightly brush the surface of the tava or frying pan with oil. Stir the batter and pour a ladleful into the middle of the griddle and quickly spread it out with the back of the ladle or a palette knife, to form a thin pancake. Don't worry if the dosa is not perfect, they are very hard to get exactly right.

4 Drizzle a little oil or ghee around the edge to help it crisp up. Cook until small holes appear on the surface and the edges start to curl. Turn over with a spatula and cook the other side. (The first dosa is often a disaster but it will season the pan for the following ones.)

5 Repeat with the remaining mixture, oiling the pan between each dosa. Roll the dosas into big tubes and keep warm. Dosas are often filled with spiced potatoes or meat and served with chutneys, or with curries.

ACCOMPANIMENTS

MANGO SALAD

SERVES 4

300 g (10½ oz) grated coconut

2 dried chillies, seeded and chopped

1 tablespoon grated jaggery or soft
  brown sugar

300 g (10½ oz) ripe mango flesh, cubed

1 tablespoon oil

½ teaspoon coriander seeds

½ teaspoon black mustard seeds

6 curry leaves

1 Put the coconut, chilli and jaggery in a blender and add enough water to make a thick, coarse paste. If you don't have a blender, crush everything together in a pestle and mortar, adding a little water as you go.

2 Transfer the paste to a bowl and toss the mango through. Season with salt, to taste, then refrigerate. Heat the oil in a small frying pan over low heat and add the coriander, mustard seeds and curry leaves. Cover and shake the pan until the seeds start to pop. Pour the oil and seeds over the mango mixture and stir.

MANGO CHUTNEY

MAKES 500 ML (17 FL OZ/2 CUPS)

1 tablespoon oil
2 garlic cloves, crushed
1 teaspoon grated ginger
2 cinnamon sticks
4 cloves
½ teaspoon chilli powder
1 kg (2 lb 4 oz) fresh or frozen ripe mango flesh, roughly chopped
375 ml (13 fl oz/1½ cups) clear vinegar
230 g (8 oz/1 cup) caster (superfine) sugar

1 Heat the oil in a heavy-based saucepan over medium heat, add the garlic and ginger and fry for 1 minute. Add the remaining ingredients and bring to the boil.

2 Reduce the heat to low and cook for 1 hour, or until the mango is thick and pulpy, like jam. It should fall in sheets off the spoon when it is ready. Add salt, to taste, and more chilli if you wish. Remove the whole spices.

3 Pour the chutney into hot sterilized jars (wash the jars in boiling water and dry them thoroughly in a warm oven). Seal the jars and allow to cool completely. Store in a cool place, or in the fridge after opening.

LACCHA

SERVES 6

1 red onion, finely sliced into rings

½ teaspoon salt

½ teaspoon cumin seeds

¼ teaspoon chilli powder

2 tomatoes, thinly sliced

450 g (1 lb) cucumbers, peeled and
thinly sliced

3 tablespoons lemon juice

1 **Mix the onion** with the salt and leave in a sieve or colander to drain for 10 minutes. Rinse under cold water, then drain and put in a bowl.

2 **Place a small frying pan** over low heat and dry-roast the cumin seeds until aromatic. Grind the roasted seeds to a fine powder using a spice grinder or pestle and mortar. Add the cumin and chilli powder to the onion and mix well.

3 **Arrange the tomato slices** on a plate and top with a layer of cucumber, then onion. Sprinkle with the lemon juice and season with salt and black pepper, to taste.

RAITA

SERVES 4

450 g (1 lb) cucumbers, grated

1 large, ripe tomato, finely chopped

310 ml (10¾ oz/1¼ cups) thick plain yoghurt

½ tablespoon oil

1 teaspoon black mustard seeds

1 tablespoon coriander (cilantro) leaves (optional)

1 Put the cucumber and tomato in a sieve for 20 minutes to drain off any excess liquid. Mix them in a bowl with the yoghurt and season with salt, to taste.

2 For the final seasoning (tarka), heat the oil in a small saucepan over medium heat, add the mustard seeds, then cover and shake the pan until the seeds start to pop. Pour the seeds and oil over the yoghurt. Serve sprinkled with the coriander leaves if you wish.

RADISH SALAD

SERVES 4

200 g (7 oz) small radishes

1 tablespoon oil

¼ teaspoon cumin seeds

¼ teaspoon black mustard seeds

pinch of asafoetida

¼ teaspoon ground turmeric

¼ teaspoon salt

1 tablespoon lemon juice

100 g (3½ oz/⅔ cup) roasted peanuts, roughly chopped

1 Use the smallest radishes that you can find for this salad. combining the radishes with peanuts gives a crunchy texture and hot flavour. It serves as a fresh-tasting accompaniment to most cooked dishes.

2 Wash the radishes and top and tail them. Cut each radish into four or eight pieces.

3 Heat the oil in a small saucepan over medium heat, add the cumin and mustard seeds, then cover and shake the pan until the seeds start to pop.

4 Add the asafoetida, turmeric and salt to the pan, then remove from the heat, add the lemon juice and leave to cool. Just before serving, arrange the radishes and the peanuts in a bowl, pour the dressing over the top and mix thoroughly.

CARROT SALAD

SERVES 4

1 tablespoon oil

¼ teaspoon black mustard seeds

¼ teaspoon cumin seeds

pinch of ground turmeric

¼ teaspoon salt

¼ teaspoon caster (superfine) sugar

1½ tablespoons lemon juice

500 g (1 lb 2 oz) carrots, finely grated

coriander (cilantro) leaves

1   Heat the oil in a small saucepan over medium heat, add the mustard and cumin seeds, then cover and shake the pan until the seeds start to pop.

2   Add the turmeric, salt and sugar to the pan, then remove the pan from the heat and leave the spices to cool for 5 minutes. Mix in the lemon juice, then toss the carrot through.

3   Cover and leave for 30 minutes. Garnish with coriander leaves just before serving.

CHURRI

SERVES 4

1 teaspoon cumin seeds

10 g (¼ oz/½ cup) mint leaves, chopped

15 g (½ oz/½ cup) coriander (cilantro) leaves, roughly chopped

2 cm (¾ inch) piece of ginger, roughly chopped

2 green chillies, roughly chopped

310 ml (10¾ fl oz/1¼ cups) thick plain yoghurt

310 ml (10¾ fl oz/1¼ cups) buttermilk

1 onion, thinly sliced

1   Place a small frying pan over low heat and dry-roast the cumin seeds until aromatic. Grind the seeds to a fine powder in a spice grinder or pestle and mortar.

2   Chop the mint, coriander, ginger and chilli to a fine paste in a blender, or chop together finely with a knife. Add the yoghurt and buttermilk and a pinch of salt to the mixture and blend until all the ingredients are well mixed. Check the seasoning, adjust if necessary, then mix in the sliced onion and the ground cumin, reserving a little cumin to sprinkle on top.

CARROT PACHADI

SERVES 4

1 tablespoon oil

1 teaspoon black mustard seeds

2–3 dried chillies

¼ teaspoon asafoetida

1 stalk of curry leaves

625 ml (21½ fl oz/2½ cups) thick plain yoghurt

4 carrots, finely grated

coriander (cilantro) leaves

1 **Heat the oil** in a small saucepan over medium heat, add the mustard seeds and chillies, then cover and shake the pan until the seeds start to pop. Remove from the heat and immediately stir in the asafoetida and curry leaves.

2 **Whisk the yoghurt** to remove any lumps, then mix in the grated carrot. Mix in the mustard seeds, chillies, asafoetida and curry leaves along with the oil, then season with salt, to taste. Garnish with coriander leaves.

KOSAMBRI

SERVES 4

50 g (1¾ oz/½ cup) moong dal

200 g (7 oz) carrots or white radish

25 g (1 oz) grated coconut

25 g (1 oz) coriander (cilantro) leaves

½ tablespoon oil

½ teaspoon yellow mustard seeds

2 dried chillies

2 tablespoons lemon juice

1 **Soak the dal** in plenty of boiling water for 3 hours, then drain.

2 **Finely grate the carrot** or radish and combine with the dal, coconut and coriander leaves in a salad bowl.

3 **Heat the oil** in a small saucepan over medium heat, add the mustard seeds, then cover and shake the pan until the seeds start to pop.

4 **Add the chillies,** remove from the heat and add the lemon juice.

5 **When cold,** pour over the remaining ingredients and toss well. Season with salt, to taste.

SWEET TOMATO CHUTNEY

MAKES 500 ML (17 FL OZ/2 CUPS)

8 garlic cloves, roughly chopped

5 cm (2 inch) piece of ginger, roughly chopped

800 g (1 lb 12 oz) tinned chopped tomatoes

310 ml (10¾ fl oz/1¼ cups) clear vinegar

350 g (12 oz) jaggery or soft brown sugar

2 tablespoons sultanas

2 teaspoons salt

¾ teaspoon cayenne pepper

chilli powder (optional)

1 Combine the garlic, ginger and half the tomatoes in a blender or food processor and blend until smooth. If you don't have a blender, crush the garlic, grate the ginger and push the tomatoes through a sieve before mixing them all together.

2 Put the remaining tomatoes, the vinegar, sugar, sultanas and salt in a large, heavy-based saucepan. Bring to the boil and add the garlic and ginger mixture. Reduce the heat and simmer gently for 1½–1¾ hours, stirring occasionally, until the mixture is thick enough to fall off a spoon in sheets. Make sure the mixture doesn't catch on the base.

3 Add the cayenne pepper. For a hotter chutney, add a little chilli powder. Leave to cool, then pour into sterilized jars (wash the jars in boiling water and dry them in a warm oven). Store in a cool place, or in the fridge after opening.

SWEETS
& DRINKS

ROSSOGOLLAS

SERVES 6

550 g (1 lb 4 oz) chenna
3 tablespoons chopped nuts (optional)

SYRUP
1 kg (2 lb 4 oz/4½ cups) sugar
3 tablespoons milk
rosewater (optional)

1 **Divide the chenna** dough into 30 portions and roll each one into a ball. If you are using the nuts, make a hollow in each ball, add a few chopped nuts to the centre, then re-roll into a ball.

2 **Make a thin syrup** by combining the sugar with 1.5 litres (52 fl oz/6 cups) water in a heavy-based saucepan and simmering the mixture over low heat until it is slightly thickened. The syrup should feel sticky and greasy. Add the milk to the boiling syrup to clarify it—this will force any scum to rise to the surface. Skim off the scum with a spoon.

3 **Drop the rossogollas** into the clean boiling syrup, reduce heat and simmer for 10 minutes, or until they float. Sprinkle a little water on the boiling syrup every 2 minutes to stop it reducing too much and foaming. When the rossogollas are cooked, they will float on the surface.

4 **Remove from the heat** and leave to cool in the syrup. For a rose flavour, add a few drops of rosewater. Keep the rossogollas refrigerated until required. Serve with a little of the syrup poured over them.

KARANJI

MAKES 30

215 g (7½ oz/1¾ cups) maida or plain (all-purpose) flour

4 tablespoons oil or ghee

oil, for deep-frying

FILLING

10 cardamom pods

100 g (3½ oz/½ cup) sugar

5 cm (2 inch) cinnamon stick

150 g (5½ oz) grated coconut

1   Sift the maida into a bowl. Add oil or ghee and rub it in with your fingers until the mixture resembles breadcrumbs. Add 5 tablespoons lukewarm water, a little at a time, and, using a palette knife, blend the dough together. Turn it out onto a floured surface and knead for 5 minutes, until smooth and pliable. Cover. Leave at room temperature for 15 minutes. Don't refrigerate or the oil will congeal, making it difficult to roll.

2   To make the filling, remove the cardamom seeds from the pods and coarsely crush them in a pestle and mortar. Combine the sugar, cinnamon and 185 ml (6 fl oz/¾ cup) water in a heavy-based saucepan. Heat gently until the sugar has dissolved. Bring to the boil, add the coconut, then stir over a low heat until the liquid has evaporated and mixture comes together. The mixture should not be bone dry. Remove from heat, add the cardamom and allow to cool.

3   On a lightly floured surface, roll out one-third of the pastry to a 28 cm (11 inch) diameter circle. Using an 8 cm (3 inch) cutter, cut out 10 circles of pastry. Place ½ tablespoon of filling in the centre of each circle, then moisten the edges with water. Seal into a semicircle and crimp the edge. Repeat until all the pastry and filling are used. Cover until ready to fry.

4   Fill a karhai or deep, heavy-based saucepan one-third full with oil and heat. Add a small piece of pastry and if it rises to the surface in a couple of seconds the oil is ready for use. Put in a few karanjis at a time and fry for about 30–60 seconds, until lightly browned. Turn them over and brown them on the other side. Remove from the pan and place on a cooling rack for 5 minutes before draining on paper towels. When cold, store in an airtight container for up to a week.

CASHEW NUT BARFI

SERVES 12

500 g (1 lb 2 oz) cashew nuts

6 cardamom pods

200 g (7 oz/2 cups) powdered milk

2 tablespoons ghee or butter

¼ teaspoon ground cloves

230 g (8½ oz/1 cup) caster (superfine) sugar

2 sheets edible silver leaf (varak), (optional)

1 Place a small frying pan over low heat and dry-roast the cashew nuts until browned all over. Cool and chop in a food processor or with a knife. Remove the cardamom seeds from the pods and crush them in a spice grinder or pestle and mortar. Line a 26 x 17 cm (10½ x 7 inch) baking tin with baking paper.

2 Combine the milk powder and cashew nuts in a large bowl and rub in the ghee until completely mixed in. Stir in the cardamom and cloves.

3 Combine the sugar and 250 ml (9 fl oz/1 cup) water in a heavy-based saucepan and heat over low heat until the sugar melts. Bring to the boil and simmer for 5–7 minutes to make a sugar syrup. Quickly stir the sugar syrup into the cashew mixture—if you leave it too long it will stiffen—and spread the mixture into the baking tin. Smooth with a buttered spatula. Place the silver leaf on top by inverting the sheets onto the surface and peeling off the paper backing. Leave to cool, then slice into diamond shapes. Serve cold.

KULFI

MAKES 12

2 litres (70 fl oz/8 cups) milk

10 cardamom pods, lightly crushed

6 tablespoons sugar

15 g (½ oz) almonds, blanched and finely chopped

15 g (½ oz) unsalted pistachio nuts, skinned and finely chopped

edible silver leaf (varak), (optional)

1 **Put the milk** and cardamom pods in a heavy-based saucepan and bring to the boil. Reduce the heat to low and simmer, stirring frequently, for about 2 hours, until the milk has reduced to a third of the original amount, about 750 ml 26 fl oz/(3 cups). Whenever a thin skin forms on top, stir it back in.

2 **Add the sugar** to the pan, simmer for 5 minutes, then strain into a shallow plastic freezer box. Add the almonds and half the pistachios, then cool. Put twelve 80 ml (2½ fl oz/ ⅓ cup) kulfi moulds or dariole moulds in the freezer to chill.

3 **Place the kulfi mixture** in the freezer and every 20 minutes, using electric beaters or a fork, give the ice cream a good stir to break up the ice crystals. When the mixture is quite stiff, divide it among the moulds and freeze until hardened completely. Dip the moulds in hot water and turn out the kulfi. Sprinkle with the remaining pistachios and decorate with a piece of silver leaf.

CARROT HALVA

SERVES 8

1 kg (2 lb 4 oz) carrots, grated

1 litre (35 fl oz/4 cups) milk

100 g (3½ oz) ghee

230 g (8½ oz/1 cup) caster (superfine) sugar

80 g (2¾ oz/⅔ cup) raisins

1 teaspoon cardamom seeds, finely ground

50 g (1¾ oz/½ cup) slivered almonds

ground cardamom

1 **Put the grated carrot** and milk in a heavy-based saucepan over low heat and bring to a simmer. Cook, stirring until the carrot is tender and the milk evaporates. This must be done slowly or the mixture will burn. Add the ghee and cook until the carrot starts to brown.

2 **Add the sugar** and cook until the mixture is thick and dry. Add the raisins, cardamom and almonds. Serve hot in small bowls, with double cream or ice cream, and sprinkle with a little ground cardamom.

GULAB JAMUNG

MAKES 24

SYRUP
440 g (15½ oz/2 cups) sugar

4–5 drops rosewater

GULAB JAMUN
100 g (3½ oz/1 cup) low-fat powdered milk

2 tablespoons self-raising flour

2 teaspoons fine semolina

2 tablespoons ghee

4 tablespoons milk, to mix

24 pistachio nuts (optional)

oil, for deep-frying

1 To make the syrup, put the sugar in a large heavy-based saucepan with 850 ml (29 fl oz/3⅓ cups) water. Stir over low heat to dissolve the sugar. Increase the heat and boil for 3 minutes. Stir in the rosewater and remove from the heat.

2 To make the gulab jamun, combine the powdered milk, flour, semolina and ghee in a bowl. Add enough milk to make a soft dough, mix until smooth, then divide into 24 portions. If using the pistachio nuts, press each piece of dough in the centre to make a hole, fill with a pistachio, then roll into a ball. If not using pistachios, just roll each piece into a ball.

3 Fill a karhai or deep saucepan one-third full with oil. Heat the oil to 150°C/300°F (a cube of bread will brown in 30 seconds) and fry the balls over low heat until golden brown all over. Remove with a slotted spoon and transfer to the syrup. When all the balls are in the syrup, bring the syrup to boiling point, then remove from the heat. Cool and serve the gulab jamun at room temperature.

ALMOND SARBAT

MAKES 250 ML (9 FL OZ/1 CUP)

250 g (9 oz/2½ cups) freshly ground
  almonds

1 kg (2 lb 4 oz/4½ cups) sugar

12 cardamom pods

almond extract, to taste

5–6 drops rosewater (optional)

1 Put the almonds, sugar and 250 ml (9 fl oz/1 cup) water in a large, heavy-based saucepan and cook over low heat, stirring constantly until the sugar dissolves.

2 Grind the cardamom with 1 tablespoon water in a pestle and mortar or spice grinder. Add to the almond syrup.

3 Stir the mixture, removing any scum from the top. Cook until the syrup thickens. Remove from the heat, strain through a sieve lined with muslin, and leave to cool.

4 Add the almond essence and rosewater, if using, and serve in long glasses, with water, over lots of crushed ice.

SALT LASSI

SERVES 4

1 teaspoon cumin seeds

625 ml (21½ fl oz/2½ cups) thick plain
   yoghurt

½ teaspoon salt

1   **Place a small frying pan** over low heat and dry-roast the cumin seeds until browned and aromatic.

2   **Blend the roasted cumin seeds** (reserve a few for garnish) with the yoghurt, salt and 310 ml (1¼ cups) water, either by hand or in a blender, and serve in tall glasses.

3   **If you would like** the lassi a little colder, add about eight ice cubes to the blender, or stir them into the blended lassi. Garnish with the reserved cumin seeds.

Note: Lassis are a very popular drink in india. they are made by blending yoghurt with a flavouring which can be either salty or sweet. both these versions are cooling, refreshing and perfect to drink with a curry.

MANGO LASSI

SERVES 4

500 g (1 lb 2 oz) ripe mango
250 ml (9 fl oz/1 cup) chilled milk
250 ml (9 fl oz/1 cup) thick plain yoghurt

1 **Chop the mango** to a pulp with a knife or in a blender, add a pinch of salt and push through a nylon sieve with the back of a spoon. Discard any fibres. The remaining syrup should be thick but should not contain any stringy bits of pulp. Refrigerate until cold.

2 **Blend the mango** with the milk and yoghurt, either by hand or in a blender. If you would like the lassi a little colder, add about eight ice cubes to the blender, or stir them into the blended lassi.

3 **If you want** to use green unripe mangoes, cook them with 220 g (7¾ oz/1 cup) sugar and a little water and add 500 ml (17 fl oz/2 cups) milk to the lassi, instead of yoghurt and milk.

MASALA CHAI

SERVES 6

2 cm (¾ inch) piece of ginger

5 cm (2 inch) cinnamon stick

4 peppercorns

3 cloves

3 cardamom pods

1 tablespoon black Indian tea

250 ml (9 fl oz/1 cup) milk

3 tablespoons sugar

1 Dry-roast the ginger under a grill (broiler) for 1 minute on each side. Put the spices and ginger in a pestle and mortar or spice grinder and roughly crush them. Put the spices, tea and milk in a saucepan with 1 litre (35 fl oz/4 cups) water and bring to the boil. Leave for 3 minutes, then add the sugar.

2 Strain off the dregs (the easiest way is to put the whole lot through a coffee plunger or very fine strainer), then pour the tea from one jug to another in a steady stream. You need to hold the jugs far apart and repeat the process until the tea begins to froth. Serve while still hot, in glasses.

MASALA COFFEE

SERVES 4

500 ml (17 fl oz/2 cups) milk

2 tablespoons sugar

2 cm (¾ inch) piece of ginger

2 tablespoons freshly ground Keralan or other coffee

5 cardamom seeds, pounded

1 cinnamon stick

cocoa powder, to sprinkle

1   Put the milk and sugar in a heavy-based saucepan, bring to the boil over low heat and keep at a low simmer.

2   Dry-roast the ginger under a grill (broiler) for 1 minute on each side, then pound it a little in a pestle and mortar to crush it and release the juices. Add to the milk with the coffee, cardamom and cinnamon. Cover and allow the flavourings to steep in the heat for 3 minutes.

3   Strain off the dregs (the easiest way is to put the whole lot through a coffee plunger or very fine strainer), then pour the coffee from one jug to another in a steady stream. You need to hold the jugs far apart and repeat the process until the coffee begins to froth. Serve while still hot, garnished with a sprinkling of cocoa.

SHRIKHAND

SERVES 4

½ teaspoon saffron strands

3 cardamom pods

250 ml (9 fl oz/1 cup) thick plain yoghurt

3 tablespoons caster (superfine) sugar

a few toasted flaked almonds

1 **Soak the saffron** in 1 teaspoon boiling water. Remove the cardamom seeds from the pods and coarsely crush them in a spice grinder or pestle and mortar.

2 **Put the yoghurt**, sugar, cardamom and saffron in a bowl and beat until well mixed. Divide among four bowls and refrigerate before serving. Serve with toasted almonds sprinkled on top.

PAYASAM

SERVES 6

100 g (3½ oz/½ cup) sago

2 tablespoons ghee

80 g (2¾ oz/½ cup) chopped or slivered
almonds

125 g (4½ oz/1 cup) sultanas

50 g (1¾ oz) sevian noodles, broken into
3 cm (1¼ inch) pieces

1 litre (35 fl oz/4 cups) milk

185 g (6½ oz/1 cup) soft brown sugar

3 tablespoons golden syrup

1 teaspoon ground cardamom

¼ teaspoon ground cloves

1 teaspoon rosewater (optional)

2 tablespoons grated coconut

1 Cook the sago in 1 litre (35 fl oz/4 cups) simmering water,
stirring occasionally, for 20–25 minutes, until the sago is clear,
then drain. Rinse and drain the sago again.

2 Heat the ghee in a heavy-based frying pan over low heat,
brown the nuts and sultanas and remove from the pan. Fry the
sevian in the same pan until light brown. Add most of the milk
and simmer the sevian until soft, stirring as it cooks. Add the
sago and remaining milk. Stir with a fork, add the sugar and
golden syrup and simmer, stirring constantly.

3 Add a little milk, if necessary, as the payasam thickens,
then add the cardamom, cloves and rosewater and stir to a
pourable consistency. Add two-thirds of the nuts and sultanas
and stir. Serve immediately or chill. Garnish with the coconut
and remaining nuts and sultanas.

APRICOTS IN CARDAMOM SYRUP

SERVES 4

300 g (10½ oz/1⅔ cups) dried apricots

3 tablespoons caster (superfine) sugar

3 tablespoons slivered, blanched almonds

1 cm (½ inch) piece of ginger, sliced

4 cardamom pods

1 cinnamon stick

4 pieces edible silver leaf (varak), (optional)

1 **Soak the apricots** in 750 ml (26 fl oz/3 cups) water in a large saucepan for 4 hours, or until plumped up.

2 **Add the sugar,** almonds, ginger, cardamom and cinnamon to the apricots and bring slowly to the boil, stirring until the sugar has dissolved. Reduce the heat to a simmer and cook until the liquid has reduced by half and formed a thick syrup. Pour into a bowl, then refrigerate.

3 **Serve in small bowls** with a piece of silver leaf for decoration. To do this, invert the piece of backing paper over each bowl. As soon as the silver leaf touches the apricots it will come away from the backing and stick to them.

FALOODA

SERVES 6

ROSE SYRUP

220 g (7¾ oz/1 cup) sugar

2 teaspoons rosewater, or to taste

pink food colouring

FALOODA

2 teaspoons agar-agar

yellow food colouring

30 g (1 oz) basil seeds

1 tablespoon icing (confectioners') sugar

1 litre (35 fl oz/4 cups) milk, chilled

6 tablespoons ice cream or thick (double/heavy) cream

pistachios, chopped (optional)

almonds, chopped (optional)

mint leaves (optional)

1 **To make the rose syrup,** put the sugar and 250 ml (9 fl oz/1 cup) water in a large, heavy-based saucepan, bring to the boil and boil for 2 minutes. Add rosewater, to taste, and enough colouring to make a pink syrup. Cool.

2 **To prepare the falooda,** dissolve the agar-agar in 250 ml (9 fl oz/1 cup) boiling water in a small saucepan. Cook over medium heat, stirring constantly for 15 minutes. Add a little yellow food colouring. Pour into a large, flat dish and refrigerate until set. Turn out onto a board and slice into thin strips (thin enough to be sucked up a straw).

3 **Soak the basil seeds** in a little water for 1 hour, then drain. Stir the icing sugar into the milk.

4 **To prepare six glasses of falooda,** pour 2 tablespoons rose syrup into each large glass. Add a helping of falooda and 2–3 teaspoons basil seeds to each and top with the sweetened, chilled milk and 1 tablespoon cream or ice cream. Garnish with nuts and mint leaves if you wish.

KHEER

SERVES 6

155 g (¾ cup) basmati rice

20 cardamom pods

2.5 litres (86 fl oz/10 cups) milk

30 g (1 oz/⅓ cup) flaked almonds

175 g (6 oz/¾ cup) sugar

30 g (¼ cup) sultanas

1　**Wash the rice**, then soak for 30 minutes in cold water. Drain well. Remove the seeds from the cardamom pods and lightly crush them in a spice grinder or pestle and mortar.

2　**Bring the milk** to the boil in a large heavy-based saucepan and add the rice and cardamom. Reduce the heat and simmer for 1½—2 hours, or until the rice has a creamy consistency. Stiring occasionally to stop the rice sticking to the pan.

3　**Dry fry the almonds** in a frying pan for a few minutes over medium heat. Add the sugar, almonds and sultanas to the rice, reserving some almonds and sultanas. Mix, then divide among bowls. Serve warm, garnished with almonds and sultanas.

INDIAN BASICS

agar-agar Also known as China grass, this is a setting agent made from certain types of seaweed. It is sold as strips, sheets, flakes or powder, dissolves in boiling water, and unlike gelatine will set at room temperature. Available from supermarkets, health food shops and Indian food shops.

ajowan (ajwain) A spice that looks like miniature cumin seeds and has a similar aroma but stronger flavour. Use sparingly.

amaranth (marsa) A leafy green, or green and dark red vegetable. It has a peppery flavour and can be substituted with spinach in recipes. Available at Indian food shops.

amchoor/amchur powder (khatai) A fine beige powder made by drying green mangoes. It is used as a souring agent or meat tenderizer in Indian cooking. Available at Indian food shops.

asafoetida (hing) This yellowish powder or lump of resin is made from the dried latex of a type of fennel. Asafoetida has an extremely pungent smell which has earned it the name 'devil's dung'. It is used to make pulses and legumes more digestible and Hindu Brahmins and Jains use it instead of garlic and onions which are forbidden to them. Asafoetida is always fried to calm its aroma. It comes in small airtight containers and is available from Indian food shops.

atta Sometimes called chapati flour, this is made from finely ground whole durum wheat. Some have a proportion of white flour added, labelled as 80/20 or 60/40. Atta is much finer and softer than wholemeal flour so if you can't find it, use half wholemeal and half maida or plain flour instead.

banana flower (kere kafool/mocha) This is the purple, teardrop-shaped flower of the banana plant. The purple leaves and pale yellow buds which grow between them are discarded. Only the inner pale core is eaten. This needs to be blanched in boiling water to remove any bitterness. Wear rubber gloves to prepare banana flower as it has a gummy substance, which can stain your fingers. Available from Indian food shops.

banana leaves Large green leaves which can be used as a wrapping (dip in boiling water to soften them) for foods, or as a plate to eat off. Young leaves are preferable. Available from Indian food shops.

basil seeds (subja) These tiny black seeds of a type of wild Indian basil are soaked in water until they swell. When soaked, they are surrounded by clear jelly. Buy at Indian food shops.

besan flour Also known as gram flour, this is a yellow flour made from ground Bengal gram or chickpeas. It has a nutty flavour and is used as a thickener in curries, as well as in batters, dumplings, sweets and breads.

bitter melon Also known as bitter gourd, karela or warty melon, this looks like a pale cucumber with a warty skin. The flesh is bitter and needs to be blanched or degorged, then married with strong flavours.

black-eyed beans (lobhia) Also called black-eyed peas, these are actually dried cow peas and are also known as chowli dal when split. They are buff-coloured beans with a small dark eye on one side. They need to be soaked overnight or pre-cooked before use. Avoid dark or wrinkled beans as they are old.

black salt (kala namak) A rock salt mined in central India. Available as black or dark brown lumps, or ground to a pinkish grey powder. Unlike white salt, it has a tangy, smoky flavour. Buy at Indian food shops.

buttermilk (chaas) Mildly sour liquid left when milk is churned to butter. Commercial buttermilk is made from fermented skim milk and is not 'live' as real buttermilk would be.

cardamom (elaichi) Dry green pods full of sticky, tiny brown or black seeds which have a sweet flavour and pungent aroma. If you need ground cardamom, open the pods and grind the seeds. Ready-ground cardamom quickly loses flavour. Use pods whole or crushed. Brown cardamom has a peppery flavour not suitable for sweet dishes.

cayenne pepper A very hot red chilli powder made from sun-dried red chillies.

chaat masala Seasoning used for various snacks known as chaat (which means 'to lick' in Hindi). The spice blend uses a variety of flavourings including asafoetida, amchoor, black salt, cumin, cayenne, ajowan and pepper.

chana dal (gram lentils) These are husked, split, polished, yellow Bengal gram, the most common type of gram lentil in India. They are often cooked with a pinch of asafoetida to make them more easy to digest.

chenna Sweetened Indian cheese, used in sweet dishes. Found in the refrigerated section in supermarkets and Indian food shops.

chickpeas (chana) Chickpeas come white (kabuli/kubli) or black (kala). The white chickpeas are actually a tan colour and the black ones are dark brown. Usually sold whole, but also sold split, dried chickpeas need to be soaked for 8 hours in cold water before use. They will double in size. Tinned ones can be used but need to be added at the end of the cooking time as they are already very soft.

chillies (lal mirch/hari mirch) Red and green chillies are widely used in Indian cuisine. Recipes generally give a colour, rather than a variety. Many varieties are grown in India and are used in a regional or seasonal context. Kashmiri chillies are dark red and mild, Goan chillies are short and stubby and mundu chillies are round. Small dhani (bird's eye chillies) are the hottest.

chillies, dried (sabat lal mirch) Dried whole chillies of various shapes, sizes and heat levels. Sometimes soaked to soften them. Remove the seeds if they are very hot.

chilli flakes Dried, coarsely ground chillies with the seeds included; usually hot.

chilli powder A wide variety of chillies are dried and crushed to make chilli powders. Some, such as Kashmiri chilli powder and paprika, are used for colour, whereas others like cayenne are used for heat. The amount used can be varied, to taste, so start with a small amount and determine how hot it is.

cloves (laung) The dried, unopened flower buds of the clove tree. Brown and nail-shaped, they have a pungent flavour, so use in moderation. Use whole or ground.

coconut (nariyal) The fruit of a coconut palm. The inner nut is encased in a husk which has to be removed. The hard shell can then be drained of juice and cracked open to extract the white meat. Coconut meat is jellyish in younger nuts and harder in older ones. Dried coconut meat is known as copra.

coconut cream This is made by soaking freshly grated coconut in boiling water and then squeezing out a thick, sweet coconut-flavoured liquid. It is available tinned.

coconut milk Thinner version of coconut cream; sold in tins.

coconut milk powder A powdered form of coconut which when mixed with water makes coconut milk or cream. Sold in supermarkets or Indian food shops.

coriander (hara dhaniya) Fresh coriander leaves are used both in recipes and also as a colourful garnish. Buy healthy bunches of green leaves. Avoid any which are yellowing.

coriander (dhaniya) seeds The round seeds of the coriander plant. The seeds have a spicy aroma, are widely used in Indian cooking and are common in spice mixes such as garam masala. To intensify the flavour, dry-roast the seeds until aromatic, before crushing them. Best freshly ground for each dish. Available whole or ground.

creamed coconut A solid block of coconut cream which needs to be reconstituted with water, or can be added straight to a dish to give a strong coconut flavour. Slice pieces off the block as required.

cumin (jeera) seeds The green or ochre, elongated ridged seeds of a plant of the parsley family. It has a peppery, slightly bitter flavour and is very aromatic. To intensify the flavour, dry-roast the seeds before crushing them. Cumin seeds are best freshly ground for each dish. Available whole or ground. Kala jeera are a black variety.

curry leaves (kadhi patta/meetha neem) Smallish green aromatic leaves of a tree native to India and Sri Lanka. These give a distinctive flavour to south Indian dishes. They are usually fried and added to the dish or used as a garnish at the end.

dal (dhal) is used to describe not only an ingredient but a dish made from it. In India, dal relates to any type of dried split pea, bean or lentil. The cooking times vary as do the texture and flavour. A dal dish can be a thin soup or more like a stew. All dal should be rinsed before use.

degchi A cooking pot which has no handle. It has a thick base to assist even cooking. .

drumsticks (sahjan) Long, dark green, ridged fibrous pods from the horseradish tree. Drumsticks, so called because of their rigidity, need to be cut into lengths before being cooked. The inner pulp, the only part eaten, is scooped out with a spoon or scraped out with your teeth. Buy uniformly slim pods. Sold in Indian food shops.

fennel (saunph) seeds The dried seeds of a Mediterranean plant, fennel seeds are oval, greenish yellow, with ridges running along them, and look like large cumin. Used as an aromatic and a digestive. To intensify the flavour, dry-roast the seeds before crushing them. Available whole or ground. Best freshly ground.

fenugreek (methi) seeds Not a true seed, but a dried legume. Ochre in colour and almost square, with a groove down one side, fenugreek has a curry aroma (it is a major ingredient in commercial curry powders) and is best dry-roasted for a few seconds before use. Don't brown them too much or they will be bitter.

garam masala A northern Indian spice mix which means 'warming spice mix', it mostly contains coriander, cumin, cardamom, black pepper, cloves, cinnamon and nutmeg. There are many versions and you can buy ready-ground mixes or make your own. Garam masala is usually added to meat dishes as a final seasoning.

ghee A highly clarified butter made from cow or water buffalo milk. Ghee can be heated to a high temperature without burning and has an aromatic flavour. Vegetable ghees are also available but don't have the same aromatic qualities. You can substitute clarified butter, or make your own ghee by melting unsalted butter in a saucepan, bringing to a simmer and cooking for about 30 minutes to evaporate out any water. Skim any scum off the surface, then drain the ghee off, leaving the white sediment behind. Leave to cool.

ginger (adrak) The rhizome of a tropical plant which is sometimes referred to as a 'root'. It is sold in 'hands'. Fresh young ginger should have a smooth, pinkish beige skin and be firm and juicy. As it ages, the skin toughens and the flesh becomes more fibrous. Avoid old ginger which is wrinkled as it will be tough. Choose pieces you can snap easily.

green banana (kela) Cooking banana, also known as plantain, which looks like a large, unripe green banana.

green unripe mango (kacha am) A variety of mango widely used for cooking in Asia. Available from Indian food shops.

hilsa (elish) A much-prized fish, this is a type of shad with sweet flesh and lots of tiny bones. Hilsa are caught when they enter fresh water to spawn. Large herrings or firm white fish can be used instead.

INDIAN BASICS

Indian bay leaves (tej patta) These are the dried leaves of the cassia tree. They look somewhat like dried European bay leaves but they have a cinnamon flavour. They are used mainly in Bengali cuisine and cuisine of the north of India.

jaggery (gur) Made from sugar cane, this is a raw sugar with a caramel flavour and alcoholic aroma. Jaggery, which is sold in lumps, is slightly sticky and varies in colour depending on the juice from which it is made. Jaggery can also refer to palm sugar. Soft brown sugar can be used as a substitute.

kalonji (nigella seeds) Small teardrop-shaped black seeds with an onion flavour, used both as a spice in northern India and as a decoration for breads such as naan.

karhai/kadhai A deep wok-shaped cooking dish. Heavy cast iron ones are best for talawa (deep-frying) and carbon steel ones for bhoona (frying). There are decorative ones which are best for serving, not cooking.

Kashmiri chilli powder Made from ground red Kashmiri chillies which have a deep red colour but little heat. A mild, dark red chilli powder can be substituted.

kokum The dried purple fruit of the gamboge tree which is used in southern Indian, Gujarati and Maharashtran cuisine to impart an acid fruity flavour. Kokum looks like dried pieces of purple/black rind and is quite sticky. It can be bought from Indian food shops and is sometimes called cocumful. A smoked version called kodampodli is also available. Kokum needs to be briefly soaked before use.

maida Plain white flour used for making naan and other Indian recipes. Plain flour is a suitable substitute.

masoor dal (red lentils) When whole (known as matki or bagali) these are dark brown or green. When split, they are salmon in colour. The split ones are the most common as they cook more easily and do not usually need soaking as the whole ones do.

methi (fenugreek leaves) The leaves of young fenugreek plants, these are used as a vegetable and treated much like spinach. They have a mildly bitter flavour. Strip the leaves off the stalks as the stalks are often tough. Spinach leaves can be used but will not give the same flavour. Available fresh or dried.

moong dal Split and skinned mung beans, which are pale yellow. The dal does not always need to be soaked. Whole mung beans (sabat moong), also called green gram, must be soaked before use.

mustard oil (sarson ka tel) Made from pressed brown mustard seeds, this is a strongly flavoured oil which is used in Bengali and Punjabi cooking. The oil is usually preheated to smoking point and then cooled to temper its strong aroma.

mustard seeds (rai) Yellow, brown and black mustard seeds are used in Indian cooking, especially in Bengal. Brown and black are interchangeable. The seeds are either added to hot oil to pop, to make them taste nutty rather than hot, or are ground to a paste before use in which case they are still hot. Split mustard seeds are called mustard dal.

oil (tel) Several types of oil are used in Indian cuisine, depending on where the dish comes from. An Indian pantry should contain several oils for different uses. Cold-pressed or refined peanut (groundnut) oil is used in northern and central India and is a good all-purpose oil (use only the refined version for deep-frying). Sesame oil made from raw sesame seeds is used in the South, and mustard oil in the Punjab and Bengal. Coconut oil is also used in the South where coconut is a major flavouring. It fries well but is very high in saturated fats.

okra (bhindi) Also known as ladies' fingers, these are green, fuzzy, tapered pods with ridges. When cut they give off a mucilaginous substance which disappears during cooking.

panch phoron (panch phora) Meaning five spices, this mix is used in Bengali and Bangladeshi cuisine. It contains fennel, brown mustard, kalonji, fenugreek, and cumin seeds in equal amounts. It can be used whole or ground.

paneer A fresh cheese made by coagulating milk with lemon juice and leaving it to drain. Paneer is usually pressed into a block and can be found in the refrigerated section in supermarkets and Indian food shops.

paprika (deghi mirch) A reddish orange powder made from ground capsicums (peppers) grown in Kashmir. Usually sweet rather than hot, paprika is used for colour. Fry it to get rid of any raw flavour. Spanish or Hungarian paprika can be substituted.

pine nuts Small cream-coloured seeds from Neosia pine cones which grow in the Himalayas. In Kashmir, they are a staple and are used both whole and ground. Any pine nut may be used.

pomegranate seeds (anardana) Sun-dried whole or ground sour pomegranate seeds, used to add a sour, tangy flavour to north Indian dishes. They are also used as a garnish.

pomfret (rupchanda, chamna) A silvery seawater fish with tiny black spots. Pomfret is expensive and hard to find outside India, although it is sometimes available frozen. Sole, flounder, leatherjacket or John Dory fillets can be substituted.

poppadom (papadam, papad, appalam) These are quite thin wafers made from a paste of lentil (gram) flours, rice flour or even tapioca or sago flour, which is rolled out very thin and then sun-dried. Poppadoms come in different sizes and flavours. Northern Indian ones often have chilli flakes or spices added. To fry poppadoms, heat about 3 cm oil in a frying pan until very hot, add the poppadoms one at a time and press them down into the oil with a spatula until they expand and lighten in colour. To flame-roast, hold one in some tongs above a gas flame until it expands in size, curls and gets flecked with bubbles (toast both sides). Fried poppadoms stay crisp for two hours.

poppy seeds (khus khus) In India, white poppy seeds are used rather than the European black or grey ones. They're used either whole or ground. The ground poppy seeds are used to thicken dishes like korma. Whole ones are often roasted and used in spice mixes. Don't use black poppy seeds as a thickener or the colour of your dish will be greyish.

puffed rice (moori, mamra, kurmura) Rather like popcorn, puffed rice is made by exploding dried rice out of its husks by dropping the grains onto hot sand. It is used in snacks such as bhel puri, or rolled in jaggery to make sweets.

rice (chaaval) Rice grain types and sizes vary across India. Much of the rice which is eaten is grown locally and it is nearly always white and polished. Popular long-grained rices include basmati, a particularly fragrant rice used for special occasions (it is expensive); patna, with a more rounded grain, is eaten in the North; and gobindavog is used in Bengal. Rices with some husk left on, which gives them some red colouration, include red patni, grown in central and western India, and rosematter, grown in southern India. You can use whichever variety you like best.

rice flour (chaaval ka atta) Finely ground rice which is used for making dosas. A coarser grind called idli-rava is used for idlis. Buy at Indian food shops.

rice sticks (rice vermicelli, chaaval ke sev) Made from rice flour, these noodles are very thin. They are used for sweets or savoury snacks and need to be softened in boiling water. Other Asian rice vermicelli can be used as a substitute.

roasted chana dal Bengal gram which have been roasted so they puff up and get a porous, crunchy texture. Used in snacks. Buy in bags from Indian food shops.

rohu A black, silvery carp with one central bone and firm flesh. It cuts well into steaksl. Any firm-fleshed fish can be substituted.

rosewater (ruh gulab/gulab jal) Made from rose essence and water, this is used to perfume sweets, desserts and drinks. It has aroma but no flavour. Use sparingly.

saag A generic term for leafy greens.

saffron strands (kesar/zaffran) The dried stigmas of a crocus flower. The strands give an intense yellow colour and musky aroma. Saffron is expensive, but only a few are needed for each dish. Soak in liquid before use.

sago (sabudhana) Small dried balls of sago palm sap which are used for milky desserts and savoury dishes. Cooked sago is transparent and soft with a silky texture.

semolina (sooj, rava) A fine, coarse or medium grain made from processed wheat with the wheat germ removed. It swells when cooked to give a creamy, textured effect. Used for sweets and quick upama.

sev Very fine noodles, used in bhel puri, made from besan flour. Sold at Indian food shops.

sevian These are very fine noodles made from wheat flour. They have a biscuity flavour. Sold at Indian food shops.

silver leaf (varak) Very thin, edible sheets of silver. They have no flavour or aroma and come in boxes or books between sheets of tissue paper. Apply the silver to the food from the backing sheet and then pull off the backing sheet. If you touch the foil, it will stick to you. Silver leaf does not go on in an even layer because it is so fragile.

split peas (matar dal) Split dried peas need to be soaked before they are cooked. They have a slightly chewy texture. Green and yellow ones are available.

tamarind (imli) A souring agent made from the pods of the tamarind tree. Sold either as a block of pulp, fibrous husk and seeds, as cleaned pulp, or as ready-prepared tamarind purée or concentrate.

tandoori food colouring A bright red powder which is used to colour tandoori dishes. Add to tandoori pastes to colour them.

tarka A seasoning process, either the first or last step, used in Indian cookery. Spices and aromatics are fried in oil to flavour the oil, then the oil is stirred into the dish at the end of cooking.

tava A specially shaped hotplate used in India to cook breads. Some are flat, others are slightly convex or concave. Keep oiled to prevent rusting. Non-stick ones are also available.

toor dal (toovar dal) Also called yellow lentils, these come oiled and plain. Oiled ones look slightly greasy and need to be soaked in hot water to remove the oil. Soak the dal for a few hours before cooking.

turmeric (haldi) Dried turmeric, sold whole or ground, is a deep yellow colour. It has a slightly bitter flavour and a pungent aroma. Turmeric is used for both colour and flavour.

urad dal The split variety (chilke urad) is a cream colour with black skin. The skinned variety is cream. Urad dal does not usually need to be soaked. The dal is used when making dosa and idli batters and it becomes glutinous and creamy when cooked.

vinegar (sirka) Made from fermented alcohol, vinegars based on sugar cane molasses (dark) and coconut (clear) are used, mainly in Parsi, Anglo-Indian and Goan food. If unavailable, substitute balsamic or white vinegar.

whole black gram (sabat urad) This whole urad dal has a black skin. Usually it has to be soaked or precooked before use.

yoghurt (dahi, doi) Yoghurt in India is made with whole milk and is a thick, set yoghurt. If you use commercial yoghurt, you may need to drain it in muslin first to remove any excess liquid.

INDEX

GREAT TASTES INDIAN